ART WORKS

PLACE

TACITA DEAN AND JEREMY MILLAR

For Mathew and Rufus
Tacita Dean

For Karen and Florence
Jeremy Millar

The authors would like to thank Lotte Møller for her invaluable help
in the research and organization of this book.

'The Thermal Stair' by W. S. Graham reprinted with permission.
Copyright W. S. Graham Estate 2005

First published in the United Kingdom in 2005 by
Thames & Hudson Ltd
181A High Holborn
London WC1V 7QX

www.thamesandhudson.com

British Library Cataloguing-in-Publication Data
A catalogue record for this book is available from the
British Library

ISBN-13:   978-0-500-93007-6
ISBN-10:   0-500-93007-4

Art direction and design by
Martin Andersen / Andersen M Studio

Printed and bound in China by C & C Offset Printing Co Ltd

CONTENTS

ENTRANCE

PLACE – THE FIRST OF ALL THINGS

'The question, what is place? presents many difficulties. An examination of all the relevant facts seems to lead to different conclusions. Moreover, we have inherited nothing from previous thinkers, whether in the way of a statement of difficulties or of a solution.'
Aristotle, *Book IV, The Physics*

Place can be difficult to locate. One might think that one can spot it somewhere, some way off in the distance, perhaps, and yet as one approaches it seems to disappear, only to reconfigure at some farther point, or back from whence one came. Place itself can seem a confusing place in which to find oneself, an uncertain place to explore, even with someone to guide us. We might be reminded of the words of the Stalker in Andrei Tarkovsky's 1979 film of the same name, the man who leads people carefully through the apocalyptic, and ever-changing, environment known as the Zone:

Our moods, our thoughts, our emotions, our feelings can bring about change here. And we are in no condition to comprehend them. Old traps vanish, new ones take their place; the old safe places become impassable, and the route can either be plain and easy, or impossibly confusing. That's how the Zone is. It may even seem capricious. But in fact, at any moment it is exactly as we devise it, in our consciousness…everything that happens here depends on us, not on the Zone.

The same is true if we begin to consider what place might be, as Aristotle observes above, although we may be more fortunate in being able to consider as guides the many thinkers who have considered the question since his time, even though they have read the intellectual terrain in many different ways. Indeed, following Aristotle (following Plato) it would seem to be difficult to find a major philosopher who has not attempted to answer the question 'what is place?', and it is a question that has been asked with increasing frequency in recent decades, as its importance is recognized in anthropology, architecture, ecology, feminism, globalism, literature, mathematics, music, psychology, urbanism – indeed, almost any area of human activity. And of course art. In this book we shall explore the theme of place in contemporary art

The People's Choice:
Kenya's Most Wanted
Komar and Melamid, 1996

The People's Choice:
Iceland's Most Wanted
Komar and Melamid, 1995

and, to help us do so, this essay will provide a brief introduction to a subject that has engaged a great many people for centuries. There is much to consider here, and we will be led in many different directions, yet we must always remember that while we might easily be lost in place, we would certainly be lost without it.

Sometimes it is assumed that we all know what 'place' means, perhaps that it even means just one thing. But as authors we would suggest that there are more concepts of place than actual geographic ones, and so certain difficulties are bound to arise. Alternately, the word might be used as a synonym for 'space' or 'location', 'site' or 'territory', as has been the case in the past, although, as we shall see, this has been for very specific reasons. One might say that 'place' is to landscape as 'identity' is to portraiture, a useful (but perhaps misused) critical term that can add distinction. It is certainly a word that is used to describe our relationship to the world around us and because, within art, this perhaps occurs most often within the genre of landscape, it is here that we should begin.

In 1993 the Russian artists Vitaly Komar and Alex Melamid began a project entitled *The People's Choice*, in which they engaged professional polling companies, compiled questionnaires and organized public meetings as a means of establishing the aesthetic judgment of 'the public', and thereby producing the 'most wanted' and the 'most unwanted' work of art. The project started in America, before expanding and considering the national 'taste' of other countries such as China and Finland, Iceland and Kenya. Interestingly, of the fifteen countries in which the project was eventually undertaken, eleven of them produced a landscape – and remarkably similar ones at that – as their 'most wanted' painting. It is interesting that landscape is not only the most popular of the major genres within the visual arts, but also the most recent, at least within the Western tradition. In much Renaissance painting, for example, the landscape is most often only glimpsed through the arches or windows of a securely interior world, or provides an exterior backdrop against which is set the main subject of the painting, often a scene taken from the Bible or the Classics. Indeed if landscape art, as we might now generally understand it, did not exist during this period, we might say that this was because landscape, as we might now generally understand it, did not exist either. Of course, this is not to say that those elements with which we are familiar within the landscape – mountains, valleys, rivers, forests – were absent from the earth, but rather that they were not considered, collectively, as landscape, and so could hardly be represented as such.

In the Dark and Middle Ages, *Landschaft*, the first form of the word, meant a collection of dwellings built within an area of cultivated land that, in turn, is surrounded by an unknown – and unknowable – wilderness. Towards the end of the Middle Ages the word was adopted by the Dutch, who transliterated it as *landschap*, although this new adaptation brought about more than a slight shift in spelling. As a small, and to a great extent man-made, country, Holland was both widely cultivated and inhabited and so such a distinction between settlements and the surrounding wilds was not only unnecessary but also, in a real sense, inconceivable. Instead, its meaning began to feel the influence of two of the most important cultural activities within Dutch cultural life and, by the seventeenth century, *landschap* came to refer to an area of land that could be represented by either surveyor or artist, as map or painting. It was at around this time that in England *landschap* became *landskip*, and it was not long before its meaning became something that we might more easily recognize: broad, often elevated, views of rural scenes in which one can see villages and fields, woods and roads. As such, it is not a natural feature of the land but rather something man-made – its organization. Indeed, this is even true when one considers those artists who later painted in the wilderness, outside the familiar areas of human modification, as the very fact of their observation –

and subsequent act of representation – transforms that which is before them into landscape. (One might even argue that a landscape ceases to exist if there is no one to look upon it.) A landscape, then, is the land transformed, whether through the physical act of inhabitation or enclosure, clearance or cultivation, or the rather more conceptual transfiguration of human perception, regardless of whether this then becomes the basis for a map, a painting, or a written account.

A landscape is the land transformed, whether through the physical act of inhabitation or enclosure, clearance or cultivation, or through human perception

Like the landscapes themselves, our understanding of landscape has changed over time, and this is true also of place. Certainly our altered understanding of place has been far more radical, and has occurred over a far greater period, and while it is beyond the scope of this short introduction to chart such momentous shifts in their full complexity, it is important that we become aware of some developments if we are to appreciate our current understanding of place and the response of contemporary artists to it.

It has become almost a commonplace, when writing upon the nature of time, to quote Saint Augustine's remark: 'What, then is time? If no one asks me, I know what it is. If I wish to explain it to him who asks me, I do not know.' In considering place, one might respond similarly. Like time, place is something with which we engage in our everyday lives; we can use it to describe the relative 'rightness' of a situation – 'A place for everything and everything in its place', as the English social reformer Samuel Smiles wrote – or a characteristic that we might appreciate, such as a 'sense of place'. Certainly, place is something more often sensed than understood, an indistinct region of awareness rather than something clearly defined. 'Place' has no fixed identity, as places themselves do not, and has similarly been subject to numerous demands, whether theological or philosophical, political or aesthetic. Indeed, the term has often been vigorously contested, as have those areas to which it refers, subject both to intellectual attack and defence, in attempts either to wrest control of it or, conversely, to despoil it, to render it of little use or value.

But how would one now enter this discussion, if asked the placial equivalent of Saint Augustine's temporal enquiry? Many of us would agree with geographer Yi-Fu Tuan's remark in 1976 that 'When space feels thoroughly familiar to us, it has become place'. Place is something known to us, somewhere that belongs to us in a spiritual, if not possessive, sense and to which we too belong. As Thomas Hardy wrote in *The Woodlanders* (1887), to belong in a place is to

know all about those invisible ones of the days gone by, whose feet have traversed the fields; …what bygone domestic dramas of love, jealousy, revenge, or disappointment have been enacted in the cottages, the mansion, the street or on the green. The spot may have beauty, grandeur, salubrity, convenience; but if it lacks memories it will ultimately pall upon him who settles there without opportunity of intercourse with his kind.

Place is thus space in which the process of remembrance continues to activate the past as

something which, to quote the philosopher Henri Bergson, is 'lived and acted, rather than represented'.

Hardy well understood the important influence of environment upon character, indeed environment *as* character, and, although a different writer in many ways, the same might also be said of James Joyce. In a preparatory note to *Ulysses*, Joyce wrote 'places remember events', and in this we can recognize how deeply time has become embedded within place, and might be said to have become one of its dominant characteristics. It is interesting to consider, for example, how many important historical events are now known simply by the name of the place in which they occurred – Hiroshima, Auschwitz, Chernobyl – although despite this, the place does not assume a dominance over the event but seems, instead, to give itself over to it wholly, as though the place can now mean little else. But place has not always been so dominated and indeed, the earliest thinkers were unequivocal in its superiority. In the fourth century BC, Archytas of Tarentum wrote a treatise on place, only fragments of which now survive:

Since everything that is in motion is moved in some place, it is obvious that one has to grant priority to place, in which that which causes motion or is acted upon will be. Perhaps thus it is the first of all things, since all existing things are in place or not without place.

For Archytas, place must take priority because it is indispensable to everything that exists, something with which Aristotle concurs, remarking in his *Physics* that 'everything is somewhere and in place'. Place is all-important because, to adapt a more recent philosophic phrase, *there is nothing outside of place.* Place is all that there is, the limit of all things and in this it might be considered as a divine being. Perhaps it is unsurprising, then, that the Hebrew name for God, *Makom*, means place; or that the first important thinker to attempt to reconcile Christianity with Greek philosophy, Philo of Alexandria, could write: 'God Himself is called place, for He encompasses all things, but is not encompassed by anything.'

It is a cruel historical irony that the very omnipresence of place could not prevent its subsequent domination by the notion of 'space', and may very well have contributed towards it. Following on from the work of Philo, another Alexandrian philosopher and theologian Johannes Philoponus worked tirelessly throughout the sixth century to challenge Aristotle on the many points where his teachings conflicted with Christian doctrine, including the definition of place. In doing so, he developed the notion of a pure dimensionality that was essentially limitless – once more, a characteristic of God alone – yet he was unwilling to develop this further into a concept of infinite space. By the late thirteenth century, however, Thomas Aquinas had demonstrated the need for such a concept and, even if he did not endorse it himself, by the time of his death in 1274, the concept of the infinite had become an imperative necessity.

In the fourteenth and fifteenth centuries, 'space' considered in its most expansive sense gradually gained precedence over what was considered the more bounded notion of place. Whereas discussions on the nature of place had initiated a consideration of limitless extension, it was 'space' that was considered most suitable for its continued exploration. In pointing towards the increased importance of infinity, place had contributed to its demise twice over: not only was

space seen as the more useful concept with which to explore the infinite, but the very things to which place seemed best suited – a sense of belonging, for example – were now considered intellectually irrelevant. The particular had been eclipsed by the universal; space had triumphed over place.

There are many places within place, many regions, each with their own identities, dialects and dialectics

Maybe this is a good place to dwell upon such matters. The first question that might be asked is do such things indeed matter? Of what relevance are the somewhat abstruse deliberations within late Hellenistic and medieval philosophy to our contemporary understanding of place in general and aspects of contemporary artistic practice in particular? It is certainly possible to consider the concept of place within contemporary art without recourse to such discussions, and many have done so, yet there are certain risks in taking such an approach. As we have already seen, place is an aggregate, the coming together of many disparate elements that can be used for many different purposes, whether it be the establishing of new intellectual foundations, or the undermining of those already extant. As such, we must recognize not only that there are fundamental differences between place and space, and between place and site, its modern replacement, but also that there are many places within place, many regions, each with their own identities, dialects and dialectics. It is a complex, ever-changing terrain – we might even consider it as a form of volcanic intellectual landscape

– one in which familiar landmarks or points of reference might shift position, become obscured by the cultural weather, or simply disappear altogether. It is important that we not only identify such things, but also remain aware of their shifts through time, as those that were once contiguous with one other another are rent apart, leaving crevices of misunderstanding into which we might otherwise fall.

The infinite space of the early modern period must have seemed overwhelming – Pascal remarked that 'The eternal silence of these infinite spaces terrifies me' – yet there were some for whom it must have offered immense possibilities rather than existential anxiety. Space offered infinite extension, and was better suited to exploring the immensities of a universe that was beginning to be revealed by Copernicus and Galileo; indeed, if the world were simply another planet orbiting the sun, then there was no reason why it should be subject to different physical laws, a shift that encouraged a greater 'universalism' in speculative thought, unbound from the particularities of place.

That is not to say that there were not fundamental differences of opinion amongst philosophers during this period over the nature of infinite space, and their disagreements continued throughout the sixteenth century, and into the seventeenth and eighteenth. Yet despite the arguments between John Locke and Isaac Newton on the one hand, both of whom supported the notion of infinite space and the void, and René Descartes and Gottfried Leibniz, who fiercely opposed it, on the other, there was a general sense of the diminishing importance of place, or rather, the importance of a diminished place. Place was absorbed within space in a distinctly subordinate role, 'a part of space' in Newton's phrase, something of 'particular limited consideration' (Locke) in contrast to the seeming unboundedness of space. Distance – and its dependency upon measurement – also contributed to the diminishing of place. This was a period of the 'mathematization of nature' whereby the world was engaged with only insofar as it could be mathematically determined. Galileo, Descartes and Locke removed what were seen as the 'secondary qualities' of place – such as colour, temperature, and texture – from their enquiries, as none of these could be converted to calculable distances and so were irrelevant to the matter in hand. As Descartes proclaimed, 'When we say that a thing is in a given place, all we mean is that it occupies such a position relative to other things.' When Leibniz makes this relationship more abstract still – the situation of things to one another, or indeed any other possible location, now becoming determinant rather than the measured distance between them – then not only does place become identical to space, but both become reduced to position or site, a 'simple location' upon the axes of analytical space. Now defined as nothing more than a position, place is unable to preserve any of the properties that were seen as inherent to it from the ancient philosophers onwards.

The fact that we are able, at the beginning of the twenty-first century, not only to conceive of a contemporary sense of place but also to testify to its cultural importance suggests that although the philosophical achievements of Descartes and Leibniz, and later Immanuel Kant, were immense, and continue to exert their influence, they were unable to raze place completely. For this we should be thankful. We retain a strong sense of place, even if we find it hard to define with any satisfaction, and this in itself demonstrates a refusal to accept the mathematical model of place-as-location proposed by such seventeenth- and eighteenth-century philosophers. As twentieth-century philosopher of science A. N. Whitehead characterized the world after Leibniz, 'nature is a dull affair, soundless, scentless, colourless; merely the hurrying of material, endlessly, meaninglessly'. This is not a form of nature that we would even recognize, much less desire, and the same is true for the artists and writers of the past three centuries or so, for whom the concept of place has been an all-important part of their work.

We retain a strong sense of place, even if we find it hard to define with any satisfaction

What is striking is that such contrasting attitudes should be at work at the very same time: while Descartes was undertaking a reclusive residence in Holland, confining himself to the warmth of his stove and a theory of mind as the self-confinement of representations, Jacob van Ruisdael was taking himself out walking in the hills and mountains of Germany, which were later presented in what have been considered by some as the first landscape paintings in oil in the West. Similarly, the poet and painter William Blake forcefully rejected the mechanistic universe of Newton, whom he portrayed as a cold monster measuring out the world, and vilified in verse: 'May God us keep / From single vision and Newton's sleep.' Another Romantic painter, Caspar David Friedrich, at work shortly after the publication of Kant's *Critique of Judgment* in 1790, demonstrated a strong conviction as to the enduring identity of place, even

Chasseur in the Forest
Caspar David Friedrich, 1813–14

to the extent that some of the people portrayed within his landscapes, such as the horseless French cavalry officer all alone in a brooding German landscape in *Chasseur in the Forest*, find themselves clearly *out of place*. The work of these artists, and many more besides, not only marks a refusal to accept the impoverishment of nature, and place, proposed by the rationalist philosophers of the period, but also puts forward a different, more generous, approach to engaging with the world. As the great English landscape painter John Constable asked in a lecture of 1836, 'Why, then, may not landscape painting be considered a branch of natural philosophy, of which pictures are but experiments?'

Little Sparta not only opens up onto the vistas of the hills beyond, but also onto vistas of memory, contemplation and understanding

Arguably the most important such artistic experiment of recent times is that established by Ian Hamilton Finlay at Stonypath, just south west of Edinburgh. Finlay moved into what was an abandoned hillside croft on an exposed desolate spot with his young family in 1966 and began work on a sunken garden and pond the following year; in doing so, he initiated the creation of one of the most celebrated gardens of the twentieth century, in which a neoclassical statue stands at rest on a tiled pathway, while a quotation from the eighteenth-century French revolutionary Saint-Just is inscribed upon large pieces of stone that act as a provocative subtitle to the Pentlands beyond. A cultivated place, the garden acts as a form of threshold, and encourages us to dwell, whether that be in the form of static contemplation, a wandering, or both. The artist Alec Finlay deftly evokes the density of the place:

To the phenomenal reality of place is added a collage of remembrances; the philosophy of Rousseau and Heraclitus, the Revolutionary ideology of Robespierre and Saint-Just, the painterly visions of Claude and Poussin, the poetry of Höderlin and Virgil, the metamorphosis of Philemon and Baucis: all are called

to bear witness. These many levels of culture and experience evoked in the garden – time, the fleeting or transitory effects of the natural world, the drama of history, the woven pattern of mythology, and the eternal verities – all are embodied in place.

In his book on Chinese gardens, Edwin T. Morris remarks that: 'A great emotional charge could be wrung from a garden that was only a few acres in physical space, but expansive in poetical space.' This is undoubtedly true of the four acres of Little Sparta, as it not only opens up onto the vistas of the hills beyond, but also onto vistas of memory, contemplation and understanding. The importance of Little Sparta to us here, then, is that as both place and art it can lead us to a greater understanding of both of these things, what we might mean by them and why they might be considered so important. Although we have become aware of how place has been perceived as in some sense 'bounded', particularly in relation to the seemingly endless extension of space, we must reconsider what

Place is perceived as in some sense 'bounded', particularly in relation to the seemingly endless extension of space

it is we mean by this, particularly as it might have some bearing on our understanding of art also. Indeed, what becomes apparent is the permeability of both concepts, as Little Sparta opens up onto its surroundings as both place and art, and so perhaps this is an important mutual characteristic. Indeed, to speak of physical limits – boundaries – in such matters is meaningless, and mistakes 'place' for 'site' and 'art' for 'art object'. It is certainly true that it is in the site, or the art object,

above and below right

**Little Sparta:
'The Present Order'**

Ian Hamilton Finlay with
Nicholas Sloan, 1983

above right

**Little Sparta: 'A Cottage, a
Field, a Plough'**

Ian Hamilton Finlay with
Nicholas Sloan, undated

that monetary value is invested, yet its greater value – spiritual, philosophical, emotional, intellectual – must be dispersed elsewhere, which is why a place or a work of art can retain a profound importance for us regardless of whether we own it or not or, indeed, whether we have seen it or not. Both place and art might be said not to contain – and be contained by – boundaries, then, but rather an innumerable series of thresholds, which extend far beyond the physical limits of either the site or the art object, and across time also, remaining even when the particular place or work of art may no longer exist. It is not that these thresholds act as points of permeability in a boundary that clearly demarcates separate elements, however, but rather as things that bring these elements together, perhaps in the manner of the bridge – itself a type of threshold – which Martin Heidegger describes as drawing the surrounding landscape together.

A place or a work of art can retain a profound importance for us regardless of whether we own it or not or, indeed, whether we have seen it or not

Writing on social spaces, the French philosopher Henri Lefebvre remarked that they 'interpenetrate one another and/or superimpose themselves upon one another', and I think that here we can substitute one term for another, and say that this is true – to some extent – for places also. We might even suggest that any single place is a process of such interpenetrations and superimpositions, whose scale, force and rhythm are engaged in an ongoing movement of shifts, rolls and waves, all of which generate new senses of place,

or new senses of the same place. 'The real voyage of discovery consists in not seeking new landscapes, but in having new eyes', Proust wrote, and perhaps these are what are required if we are to see the complexities of the places that surround us. In doing so, we would see that these different senses of place are often in conflict with one another, with those holding a particular understanding of a place feeling it necessary to eliminate a competing claim. Lefebvre is perhaps more optimistic here, remarking that 'the local…does not disappear, for it is never absorbed by the regional, national or even worldwide level. The national and regional levels take in innumerable "places"; national space embraces the regions; and world space does not merely subsume national spaces, but even (for the time being at least) precipitates the formation of new national spaces through a remarkable process of fission.' While we would not suggest that the direction of power and influence is always exerted from the larger to the smaller, from the national to the local – the very sense of a nation is often a creation of its accumulated local parts – it is certainly true that it is the local which is most often sacrificed for the 'national good', a concept that is most often defined in relation to other nation states and the 'necessities' of the 'global market'. It is within the local that international airports are built, for example, or rivers dammed, or oil fields drilled (place becomes simply a resource, a 'standing-reserve' in Heidegger's phrase). If place is viewed simply as site, its 'secondary qualities' denied, then it becomes easier to destroy it; one cannot mourn what one denied ever being in existence. There are many people who value, and fight to protect, the particularities of place, however, although within a society which often operates on a principle of economic utility, the calculable 'benefits' presented by developers, investors or corporations are often more easily grasped than the more intangible 'sense of place', with its related notions of authenticity, character and identity. Perhaps what is required is a new sense of necessity; as the early Taoist philosopher Chuang-Tse remarked, 'Everybody knows that the useful is useful, but nobody knows that the useless is useful too.' Here, too, we may have discovered something else that both place and art have in common.

Artists are not bound in the same way that property developers are, and so have no need to build upon what is already in place

Art, like place, is a process of accumulation and seldom calls for the active destruction of that which came before. It is often said that artists 'build upon' the art that came before them, but it is an unfortunate phrase. Artists are not bound in the same way that property developers are, and so have no need to build upon what is already in place. The art they create may open up onto the art created by others – as Finlay's opens up onto Claude and Poussin, for example – but it has no need to take its place, or to deny it. Even art that adopts a critical position in relation to the art or thinking of the past acknowledges the existence of that which came before (indeed, its own position is dependent upon it). In the late 1960s the American conceptual artist Douglas Huebler created a number of works as part of his *Duration* and *Location* series that, with a certain dry humour, explored how we perceive, and represent,

time and place. A work he made as a multiple is typical of his practice:

Location Piece #2
New York City – Seattle, Washington

In New York and Seattle an area was arbitrarily selected within which a person in each city photographed places that he, or she, felt could be characterized as being (1) "frightening" (2) "erotic" (3) "transcendent" (4) "passive" (5) "fevered" (6) "muffled".

Within each area each person made two entirely different sets of six photographs after which all four sets were sent to a third person (the artist) with no information that would make it possible to key any one of the photographs with any one of the words originally specified. The four sets (24 photographs) were then scrambled altogether and 12 of these arbitrarily selected for this piece; to those were added 4 photographs that had not been made to characterize any kind of place.

16 photographs, a Xerox map of New York and another of Seattle join with this statement to constitute the form of this piece.

Douglas Huebler
July, 1969

Huebler's statement may be a simple description of the process of making the work, yet it tells us also about artists' changing relationship to the landscape. The first thing that we notice is that the title, *Location Piece #2*, sits above two different locations, separated by the vast width of the American continent; the arbitrary selection of the sites, and the fact that it is two anonymous people – one in each city – rather than Huebler himself, who will be taking the photographs, further diminishes

Location Piece #2
Douglas Huebler, 1969

any sense of profound engagement between artist and place. The instruction given to each person to photograph a place that they felt could be characterized in a certain way relates clearly to a Romantic notion that the critic John Ruskin called the 'pathetic fallacy', the belief that the landscape might be made to mirror the emotional state of the person found within it. Usually, these states were ones of great turmoil, melancholy or despair, depicted by violent storms, deep chasms or overhanging rocks, the great motifs of the natural sublime, and Huebler's list begins in the same Romantic vein, requesting that photographs be taken of places 'frightening', 'erotic' and 'transcendent'.

But what of 'passive', and then his final term, 'muffled'? Our expectations are here being undermined, something that becomes even clearer when we read, in the second paragraph of Heubler's statement, of the arbitrary process of selection – and addition – that he then undertook in order to arrive at the complete set of sixteen photographs. However, the artist's activities do not prevent us from attempting to reconnect mentally the pictures – and places – with the characteristics described. And yet do we feel frightened, transcendent, or erotic? Not in the least. But despite expectations, we do actually feel rather passive when faced with these small and rather banal black-and-white photographs, and our emotional response is somewhat muffled. With great simplicity, Huebler has created a rich and delicate work that asks us to consider the difference between what we believe to be our relationship to a landscape, and what we would like to believe that relationship to be. Such a difference characterizes another quality that Huebler might have chosen – integrity – a quality that has a profound impact upon any understanding of place.

In Huebler's work, the commonplace is utterly transformed, the most banal view afforded the potential for immense significance. Perhaps it is no coincidence that it was made during the period of the first lunar landing, a period in which the most barren view was given the most poetic name and photographs of footsteps in strange colourless dust became symbolic of manifest destiny and the greatest of human achievements. Huebler's contemporary, Robert Smithson, made photographs that possessed a similar sense of detachment. His photo-text work *A Tour of the Monuments of Passaic, New Jersey* (1967), which was published in the American magazine *Artforum*, consists of photographs of various 'monuments' on the bank of the Passaic River, along which a new highway was being built, and a narrative commentary that describes this return to his birthplace a few months before his thirtieth birthday. Yet there is no attempt here to reconstruct the places of his childhood, but rather to make them seem even more strange, more dislocated temporally – in either the distant past or future – or as simply unreal, like a picture already, as when he describes his activities as 'like photographing a photograph'. In this extraordinary work, as in so many others, Smithson photographed the earth as though it were an alien environment, his birth town as if it were another planet, an environment that he was placing under a series of experiments, testing its physical and conceptual parameters, one against the other: testing it as place. In the twelfth century, Hugo of St Victor wrote: 'The man who finds his country sweet is only a raw beginner; the man for whom each country is as his own is already strong; but only the man for whom the whole world is like a foreign country is perfect.' This is not to deny the possibility or importance of a connection to a particular place, but

Ariana
Marine Hugonnier, 2002

rather to maintain a sense of active engagement with it, rather than succumb to the complacency of familiarity. This was one of Smithson's great achievements, and the achievement also of any number of other contemporary artists, some of whom we have been able to include in this book, such as Dan Graham or Joachim Koester, Doug Aitken, or Jane and Louise Wilson, Roni Horn or Alexander and Susan Maris, Graham Gussin or Mette Tronvoll. What is it that these (often very different) artists share in their relationship both to art and to place? Perhaps an answer might be found within, or suggested by,

A more profound engagement must depend upon more than the visual, upon those things that remain invisible

another recent work, by the French artist Marine Hugonnier. In her film *Ariana*, we hear the voice of the filmmaker (who may or may not be the artist) describe a visit made to Afghanistan with a small crew ('the anthropologist, the geographer, the cameraman, the sound engineer and the local guide') in order to film a panoramic view of the Afghan landscape. Denied access to the mountain ranges that would provide the vantage point for such a shot – these are strategic points, more often used to gain military, rather than representational, mastery over the surrounding area – the film becomes an exploration into the problematic nature of this form of representation. By this we do not mean the problems of access or permission, which are eventually resolved, but rather those of representation itself, which it is far more difficult to overcome. When the crew are finally allowed to gain a vantage point above the city, from the appropriately named 'Television Hill', we see a view over the city towards the distant mountains and are told that: 'The entire landscape was like a still image, a painting./ This spectacle made us euphoric and gave us a feeling of totality.' The crew could not claim mastery of what they saw, however, and remained invisible; instead we see the Afghan soldier who accompanied them and 'stood proudly in front of the view'. The filmmaker recognized the failings of what they were doing. 'We gave up filming', she says, and the screen goes black.

We would suggest that the filmmaker comes to recognize something that many of the artists included in this book have recognized too, and that is the profound limitation of the visual. This might seem a perverse thing to write in the introduction of a book on visual art, and yet why should it be so? Surely nobody is more aware of the limitations of the visual than visual artists, just as poets are most sensitive to the inadequacies of language. That such considerations have emerged during an enquiry into 'place' is perhaps not surprising, as here too the visual attains a certain prominence without ever being able to engage fully with the subject. Just as we may derive visual pleasure from looking at a particular picture, or a particular landscape, a more profound engagement must depend upon more than the visual, upon those things that remain invisible. How would one make visible the extraordinary history and mythic status of the Bialowieza Forest in eastern Europe? Perhaps we cannot, which may be why such places are often so threatened; they look just like many other places if we cannot see 'the invisible ones of the days gone by', in Hardy's phrase. And yet this does not deny its importance nor, by extension, the importance of

the photographs made by Joachim Koester of this place (see pages 90–93). Or consider the photograph by Guy Moreton of all that remains of Ludwig Wittgenstein's house overlooking Lake Eidsvatnet in Norway, part of an ongoing collaborative project with Alec Finlay that considers the relationship between the great Austrian philosopher and his frequent self-imposed exiles in such places. ('I am not interested in constructing a building, so much as in having a perspicuous view of the foundation of possible buildings.' – Wittgenstein.) They are both beautiful works of art, certainly, as the forest is, as the fjord is, and they invite our attention, yet they are both so much more than what we can see. Perhaps this is why

art, like place, needs a little time, a little patience, and no little sensitivity, in order that we might then become aware of what else it is, beyond that of which we are first aware. Not that every place that is made is art, however; but to make art (which is also to think about it) is to make place. There are many types of place, as there are many types of art, and in looking at them now, thinking about them, many more will be made. 'Everything is somewhere and in place', Aristotle said, and while our means are necessarily too modest to be quite so all-inclusive, we hope that what we have gathered here will encourage you to dwell a little upon this rich, enduring, bewildering subject. At the very least, it is a good place to start.

'The difficulties that we run into are like those we would have with the geography of a country for which we have no map, or only a map of isolated places.... We may freely wander about within the country, but when we are compelled to make up a map, we get lost. The map will show different roads which lead through the same country and of which we could take any one at all, but not two.'

Ludwig Wittgenstein

URBAN

For most of us, the city is the backdrop to our lives. Familiar and yet sometimes sinister, the streets are at once the site of social interaction and something darker, something more violent. But as cities grow, they begin to resemble one another, becoming an ever-expanding mass. What does this do to our sense of place, and our sense of ourselves? Do we connect to them in new ways? Do we live in an accumulated city, the collected memory of all the cities we have known? To live in the city, must we assume the position of the anonymous stranger?

The American artist Doug Aitken has created a number of visually stunning – and often formally complex – video installations that use a place, and its history, as a point of departure. From this starting-point, a journey might begin, over greater or lesser distances, and of greater or lesser durations. In *Monsoon* (1995), Aitken visited Jonestown, Guyana, where on 18 November 1978 followers of Reverend Jim Jones committed what was said to be an act of mass suicide. Although this dramatic event is referred to at the opening of the video, what follows is a series of quiet observations – a delicate red flower, for example, or the rusting chassis of an upturned truck – made while the artist awaited the arrival of a monsoon. It is these dark clouds, rather than those of a turbulent history, that we can see approaching, although the rain, and the sense of relief it might bring, never comes. *Eraser* (1998) also makes use of a formal structural device, albeit one that does not overdetermine what might be found within it. Here Aitken walked a straight line – from north to south – across the island of Montserrat, which had been devastated by a volcanic eruption the previous year. The viewer is invited to share this journey, to travel with this artist across a catastrophic landscape, settling upon – if not within – abandoned houses or an empty chapel. While the camera – and the viewer – can only settle upon that which remains, the buildings, it is that which no longer remains – namely, human inhabitation – that is most keenly felt.

The relationship between place and its inhabitants, and the characteristics they share, is most explicitly explored in *Electric Earth*, a complex eight-screen installation through which the viewer moves, following the journey of its protagonist, played by Ali Johnson, as he makes his way through a deserted nocturnal landscape of satellite dishes, laundromats and shopping malls. Aitken imagined this character as being the last person on earth, an earth now populated by machines, the movements of which – pulsing, spasmodic – appear to take over his body, effacing the line that divides the natural and the mechanical. *Electric Earth* is a post-Romantic vision of perfect coincidence between a human and his surroundings, although one in which it is now the human who is the projection of the electrified landscape.

'Uprooting and removal surrounds us, and at times these can be mirrored in our working process. At times I just let go and am assimilated into my landscapes, other times I feel an active resistance. I think there's something about growing up in America that makes you feel nothing is ever really stationary. Home can be motion at times.'

'I don't feel these works necessarily take places as if they were documents, unearthing them and bringing them to the table for examination. If I'm presenting data it's without resolution…to question and not to conclude.'
Doug Aitken

Electric Earth
Doug Aitken, 1999

'Copacabana has no centre. No ties to the golden youth...a sort of oasis.'

from the soundtrack of Plages

'A neighbourhood's architectural distinctiveness has in itself an effect on group identity. Through day-to-day visual experience the inhabitants of a neighbourhood know when and where they have crossed the line from a region that is "us" to a region that is "them".... Any sharply circumscribed town can thus be a unifying landmark for its inhabitants. It performs this role by simply being there for everyone to see and experience. A town favoured with architectural monuments enjoys the added advantage of symbolic resonance – a resonance that is further heightened when ceremonies are conducted around them and stories are told about them.'

Yi-Fu Tuan

Plages (2001) is the third in a loose trilogy of films by the French artist Dominique Gonzalez-Foerster that explore the felt experience of time within an urban setting. In *Riyo* (1999) we move slowly and smoothly down a Japanese river, people meeting one another below the façades of buildings lit up in the early evening twilight. We hear a phone ring, and a flirtatious conversation begins between a man and the caller, a young woman called Riyo. The conversation turns to recent memories and future hopes, and the separation of geography, and all the while the world slips slowly by, imbued with these new possibilities as both time and water continue their inexorable flow. There is water too in *Central* (2001), in which a woman dressed entirely in black looks out from the Star Ferry Terminal in Hong Kong as she awaits the arrival of her brother. As people perform their morning stretches, or look out in silent contemplation, a voice over remarks: 'Now is a moment without limits. Everything begins anew. Everyone carries his own space around. Does his own little dance. It's the present.'

This might remind us, in turn, of *Plages*, a fifteen-minute film shot from a hotel room in Rio de Janeiro overlooking the Copacabana beach. Under a darkening sky, crowds of people – often dressed in white – gather upon the beach and surrounding garden, illuminated by the chemical light of street lamps or the more intimate glow of beach fires. The camera moves along the black-and-white wave-patterned pavement and the people along it become patterns too; no longer individuals, this is a portrait of a group experience, of a public space in which the public itself is made manifest. On the soundtrack – an accumulation of fireworks, music and voices – we hear: 'If there is one place where mankind's utopia exists…Copacabana must be that place.' As the crowd continues to move along the wave pattern, we hear a last statement, delivered by a local fisherman: 'Copacabana is wonderful. It's a wonderful city. Copacabana doesn't exist.'

Plages
Dominique Gonzalez-Foerster, 2001

Et cela s'est passé à Copacabana.

Jane and Louise Wilson have often used place as a character within their video installations, an architectural protagonist that, far more than being merely a setting for what occurs within it, actually shapes it, influences it, perhaps even determines it. *A Free and Anonymous Monument* is their most ambitious and expansive work to date, and explores a number of different places in their native north-east of England, rather than a single place – or building – as in their earlier works shot in the decommissioned nuclear base at Greenham Common in Wiltshire, or the mysterious headquarters of the Stasi, the secret police of the former East Germany. It is also their most expansive piece with regards to its presentation: the images are projected upon a number of screens that surround the viewers, hanging around and above them in a manner reminiscent of the suspended constructions of the British artists Richard Hamilton and Victor Pasmore that had been exhibited at the Hatton Gallery in Newcastle in 1957. A more explicit reference to Pasmore is made in a sequence showing the Apollo Pavilion, which was designed by the artist for the new town of Peterlee, outside Gateshead. A gesture of hope for a new community, the pavilion soon became derelict, the water that surrounds it greasy and stagnant. Upon visiting the pavilion years later Pasmore remarked that the graffiti that defaced his original murals and now covered the structure 'humanised it and improved it more than I ever could'. No doubt there was a degree of bitterness at the failure of another utopian project, however; while a local councillor tried to get the Territorial Army to blow it up, Pasmore suggested that the problem of the pavilion could be solved by blowing up the neighbouring houses instead.

The installation resonates with other places, other histories, too. We see the abandoned multi-storey car park in Gateshead that played its part alongside Michael Caine and Ian Hendry in Mike Hodges' film *Get Carter* (1971), and oil rigs out at sea, but also visions of the new north-east, the North Tyneside factories that make computer chips, part of the regeneration of the region following the collapse of shipbuilding and heavy industry in recent decades. If all of the Wilsons' art has been about a sense of place, then this work more than any other suggests that such a sense is made up from the intersection of many things and the spaces between them through which we can move and find ourselves.

The effect that places can have upon our social interaction has been an important area of enquiry for British artist Liam Gillick. From the tunnels under the White House in which take place imagined conversations between former US Secretary of Defense Robert McNamara and Director of the RAND Institute, Herman Kahn, in his film *McNamara* (1994), to the beach, house and basement – each drawn by the artist's mother – that provide potential scenarios for his extended work *The What If? Scenario* (1996), Gillick adopts certain places for his own ends, re-imagining them as active participants in an ongoing discourse that will, in turn, bring about new forms of place. The photographs that make up *Pain in a Building* – the title echoing a phrase from another of Gillick's architecturally inflected works, *Big Conference Centre* (1998) – were taken at Thamesmead, a 1960s housing estate on the outskirts of London that had a clearly utopian social vision, although it is perhaps more recognizable as the location for a number of scenes within Stanley Kubrick's dystopian film *A Clockwork Orange*. Throughout the film, the estate's future was in a sense accelerated, prematurely aged, its flaws revealed before they had developed in actuality (perhaps the film simply made actual what the estate itself kept in potential, the disintegration of the cluster of social beliefs that had brought it about). As in his more recent works, which make more explicit reference to utopian models of thought – such as *Literally No Place* (2002), which explores the nature of a commune based upon B. F. Skinner's 1948 novel *Walden 2* – Gillick has created an area of engagement, a discursive space, in which we might consider what it is for art to be *topical* – that is, related both to location and events.

'80 slides and 4 soundtracks form a location shoot for a potential movie to be written by Liam Gillick and Thomas Mulcaire, directed by Philippe Parreno and produced by Anna Sanders Films, Paris. The images were taken at Thamesmead in South London. The construction of Thamesmead began in the late 1960s and formed the location for the film A CLOCKWORK ORANGE. The film was pulled from distribution in Britain after only a short release period. Kubrick was concerned that the vision of Britain portrayed in the film would encourage violence and social unrest.'

Liam Gillick

this page and opposite
Pain in a Building (details)
Liam Gillick, 1999

Dan Graham's artistic practice grew from relationships with a number of artists – including Sol LeWitt, Donald Judd and Robert Smithson – whom he had exhibited while manager of the John Daniels Gallery on 68th Street in New York. Sharing many of the same conceptual interests as these artists – in particular a reconsideration of the nature of art and its institutions – he began to make works to appear in magazines, thereby exploring the non-commodified nature of much contemporary practice, while emphasizing the importance of engagement with the social arena. Graham had been taking photographs of suburban housing in New Jersey since late 1965, some of which were exhibited in 'Projected Art' at Finch College in November 1966, and when *Arts Magazine* offered to published the photographs (at Smithson's suggestion), Graham agreed, although he decided also to write a short critical essay on the systemic permutations of the new suburban housing, the photographs now becoming illustrations to the text. Graham produced a dummy layout for the article (reproduced here) although when it was published in the December 1966–January 1967 issue of the magazine, the layout was altered; ironically, Graham's photographs were removed, and his text was accompanied by an illustration from one of the housing companies referred to, and a photograph by Walker Evans, whose deadpan style Graham had himself appropriated for his own conceptual ends. While the photographs and the rather dry, analytical text might seem to emphasize the artificiality of these suburban developments – a 'synthetic order', Graham wrote, that is 'without roots' – Graham suggests that these are also places of everyday hopes and pleasures.

'There is no organic unity connecting the land site and the home. Both are without roots – larger parts in a larger, predetermined, synthetic order.... This serial logic might follow consistently until, at the edges, it is abruptly terminated by pre-existing highways, bowling alleys, shopping plazas, carhops, discount houses, lumberyards, or factories.'

Dan Graham, from Homes for America

'The crowd is his element, as the air is that of the birds and water of fishes. His passion and his profession are to become one flesh with the crowd. For the perfect *flâneur*, for the passionate spectator, it is an immense joy to set up house in the heart of the multitude, amid the ebb and flow of movement, in the midst of the fugitive and the infinite. To be away from home and yet to feel oneself everywhere at home; to see the world – such are a few of the slightest pleasures of the independent, passionate, impartial natures which the tongue can but clumsily define. The spectator is a prince who everywhere rejoices in his incognito.'
Charles Baudelaire

The work of the young Bosnian artist Bojan Sarcevic often explores our relationship to place, in its political, poetic and personal senses, although actually it might be more accurate to describe the works as explorations of displacement. His homemade, phonetically transcribed *Zurvival Guid* (2002) is written in the kind of Pidgin English spoken by autodidacts the world over, those who have learned the language through the mass media of TV, advertising, films or music, or conversations made possible by mass-market tourism:

'It iz no uze giving up. Onli positiv aktions kan save yu. Pipol kan zurviv simingly impozibl zituations if dey hav ze determinations.'

While it is true that a certain amount of subtlety is lost in Sarcevic's invented language, there is no doubt that a greater amount of communication is gained, a degree of understanding that could prove useful when one finds it difficult to comprehend one's surroundings. Perhaps the same is true for his video *Untitled (Bangkok)*, which, similarly, highlights the relationship between different forms of experience. In this work, the artist makes his way on foot through the streets and passageways of the Thai capital, a city that has become a popular tourist destination, no doubt for the very reason that it can offer something 'other' to those who go there, particularly from the west. But the tourists are themselves also 'other' to the city's inhabitants, and as he moves through their familiar terrain, a walking sign of difference, Sarcevic seems invisible, his movements – and the recording of them – passing unnoticed by those around him.

Untitled (Bangkok)
Bojan Sarcevic, 2002

> 'Something is uncanny – that is how it begins. But at the same time one must search for that remoter "something" which is already close at hand.'
>
> *Ernst Bloch*

For the Canadian artist Stan Douglas, landscape is never simply the backdrop to history, or merely its witness, but also an active participant in its creation. In his single-channel video installation *Nu•tka•* (1996), for example, we see a classically beautiful view looking out over Nootka Sound, on the west coast of Vancouver Island, and now the site of prolonged battles over the proposed clearing of virgin forest. It had also been the site of a much earlier conflict, between the indigenous people of the region and the English and Spanish explorers, both of whom had ambitions to claim the region for their respective nations. The Nootka people themselves are not heard in this work; the soundtrack consists solely of the troubled thoughts of both English Captain and Spanish Commander, just as the image is split, divided by the alternate raster lines of the video image. The European claims upon the land – often supported by the surveying panorama mimicked here – are broken in two and rendered incomplete.

Douglas is also fascinated by the gothic – at one point, the two narrators in *Nu•tka•* quote from Poe's *The Fall of the House of Usher* in unison – and this fascination is also visible in a more recent work *Le Détroit*. In this six-minute film, we follow a young black woman as she searches in an abandoned house for something that remains a mystery to us, a short story that alludes to the novel *The Haunting of Hill House* (1959) by Shirley Jackson, while Douglas also draws individual motifs from the *Legends of Le Détroit* edited by Marie Hamlin in 1884. The film is projected onto semi-transparent material, while its negative is projected – with a small time interval – upon the screen's reverse, thereby emphasizing the haunting nature of the narrative, while alluding to the social and racial divisions that have led to so much conflict and dilapidation in what was once so prosperous a city.

Le Détroit
Stan Douglas, 1999–2000

'The perfect symmetry between the dismantling of the Wall of shame and the end of limitless Nature is invisible only to the rich Western democracies. The various manifestations of socialism destroyed both their peoples and their ecosystems, whereas the powers of the North and the West have been able to save their peoples and some of their countrysides by destroying the rest of the world and reducing its peoples to abject poverty. Hence a double tragedy: the former socialist societies think they can solve their problems by imitating the West; the West thinks it is the sole possessor of the clever trick that will allow it to keep on winning indefinitely, whereas it has perhaps already lost everything.'

Bruno Latour

Bantar Gebang, Bekasi, West Java, May 2000
Jeroen de Rijke / Willem de Rooij, 2000

It was in 1978, two years after beginning his studies under the influential photographer Bernd Becher at the Academy of Fine Arts in Düsseldorf, that German artist Thomas Struth began work on a series of photographs of cities, or rather of city streets. Perhaps influenced by his new teacher, many of Struth's photographs from this period followed a relatively strict formal method: the photographs are taken in the middle of the road (which often necessitated them being taken early in the morning, when there was less traffic) with the camera placed horizontally and at or above eye level. The resultant pictures share certain characteristics as a consequence: a strict linear perspective emphasized by the symmetrically receding façades of the buildings, a patch of cool grey sky at the centre (the pictures were black and white during this early period). What is interesting about such an approach is that by adopting the same compositional structure for each photograph, and thereby ignoring the specifics of each place, we are able to compare the photographs more easily, thereby allowing the specifics of each place to emerge perhaps more clearly than might otherwise have been the case. For all their similarities, then – and together it is possible to see these cities as part of a pan-global urbanism – it is clear that the photographs of Edinburgh could not have been taken in New York, just as the photographs of New York could not have been taken in Edinburgh or Tokyo or London.

Struth did not use this compositional device exclusively for long, however. He soon allowed the places themselves to suggest the manner in which they might be photographed. Other series followed: portraits, often of friends, fellow artists and their families; museum interiors, in which viewers often seem to fall into dynamic relationships with the spaces (and the people that inhabit them) in front of the paintings and sculptures; intimate studies of flowers; and larger landscape works, often of forests or other seemingly natural environments, which are collected under the title *Paradise*, thereby suggesting that they possess a cultural function, even if it is only one of mental escape. Yet despite their various subject matters, Struth's photographs always seem to possess a clarity of enunciation, an *intelligence* we might call it. Perhaps it is the very 'situatedness' of the pictures that allows them to find their own place irrespective of these aesthetic categories.

Jiangxi Zhong Lu, Shanghai
Thomas Struth, 1996

'All things on earth, and the earth as a whole,
flow together into a reciprocal accord.'
Martin Heidegger

NATURE

Nature is a cultural construct, a place that feeds the urban imagination as much as the urban belly. It is here that we are said to find ourselves, our 'true nature'. Yet we are increasingly unaware of how to read the terrain and are blind to the many changes and marks that our predecessors have made to the land over the centuries. To wander across cultivated fields is to encounter the earliest forms of human activity. Even those places that remain unaltered by humankind, areas of pristine wilderness, have become the crowded habitat of our cultural minds, from writers and poets to artists.

Huang Shan, Huang Shan
Thomas Struth, 2002

'As we turn every corner of the Narrow Road to the Deep North, we sometimes stand up unawares to applaud and we sometimes fall flat to resist the agonizing pains we feel in the depths of our hearts. There are also times when we feel like taking to the roads ourselves, seizing the raincoat lying near by, or times when we feel like sitting down till our legs take root, enjoying the scene we picture before our eyes.'

Soruyō

The influence of the natural world upon our sense of identity – both national and personal – and upon the production of art is well acknowledged; however, it must also be acknowledged that both the sense of identity and the art thus produced does, in turn, influence our relationship with and understanding of the natural world, thereby creating a rich area for exploration. The Norwegian artist A. K. Dolven has often drawn upon such complex relationships in her sparse and poetic videos, and has, in works such as *portrait with cigarette* or *puberty* (both 2000) made particular reference to the paintings and prints of Edvard Munch (1863–1944), which play such an important role in Norway's sense of self. Her three-screen video installation *looking back* does not make explicit such a point of reference, however, although it does share a similarly profound relationship between people and their surroundings, a relationship that can seem both calm and uncertain. Here we see three large video portraits of three women projected side by side, each seen against magnificent mountain scenery. Like the landscape itself, the women seem to move with a glacial slowness, their expressions ambivalent. Looking over their shoulders, the women begin to walk backwards, hesitantly at first but then with increasing confidence, until they pass across and out of the frame.

'Like a dream image that continues to haunt you on the other side of waking, *looking back* blurs the line dividing one state of reality from another. Here, in this valley in the far north of Norway, so close to zero in temperature and latitude, it is almost as if we, too, had crossed an invisible threshold into a numinous looking-glass world, an enchanted hyperborean landscape where the roles of everyday logic are suspended or sent into reverse.'
Steven Bode

this page and opposite
looking back
A. K. Dolven, 2000

'Island for Weeds (Prototype)

Originally conceived to float on Loch Lomond, Scotland, within the newly-established Scottish National Park, *Island for Weeds* is a support structure designed to sustain and contain a small number of *Rhododendron ponticum* plants. It is part of an ongoing body of work that focuses on the introduction and subsequent demonization of this hardy shrub. The name *ponticum* comes from the Pontus Hills in Turkey, but the plant is indigenous to many parts of the Caucasus and the southern Mediterranean. It was first introduced into Britain in 1756 from the hills overlooking Gibraltar on the southern tip of the Iberian Peninsula. From its prized position in many British ornamental gardens, it soon escaped into the wild and established itself as a strong force among the indigenous flora. While admired for its flamboyant spring blooms and still featured in many a picturesque image of the Scottish landscape, *Rhododendron ponticum* has become a major problem for landowners and conservationists alike. Its presence in the National Park poses fundamental questions in relation to the nature and make-up of the country's landscape – questions finally considered to be too contentious to be addressed by a public art work.

   Island for Weeds is designed around a number of plastic pipes of the type most commonly used for gas mains under the road. Due to their fatigue-resistant characteristics they are also increasingly deployed in marine engineering and fisheries. The system is designed in such a way that it can regulate its own height in the water using compressed air stored in the dark blue pipes and varying amounts of water stored in the yellow tanks causing the island to rise back to the correct level. The system is maintained from time to time by topping up the dark-blue pressurized pipes with a scuba tank.'

Simon Starling

Island for Weeds (Prototype)
Simon Starling, 2003

'Nature is still elsewhere.'
Ralph Waldo Emerson

this page and opposite
Moss valley series (details)
Olafur Eliasson, 2002

'Nature, in the work of Eliasson, is hardly without identity: it is, on the contrary, mired in the image of his native Iceland, its fog, moss, steam and ice, and flowing waters scattered around the world as so many emblems of a marginal piece of wilderness we take to be both personal and exotic.'
Ina Blom

In the nineteenth century, the polar regions were seen as almost abstract spaces, empty and white, upon which human hopes and fears could be projected (in this sense, they operated in a manner comparable to the moon, or outer space, during much of the twentieth century). But whereas writers as diverse as Charlotte Brontë and Edgar Allan Poe, Elizabeth Gaskell and Jules Verne, and even Emily Dickinson, have used the icy expanses, it is interesting that there is little great polar visual art. In part this is due to the technical difficulties of making pictures in such an inhospitable environment, but perhaps the greater problems are conceptual: in the featureless expanses of the poles, the conventions of representational landscape art are rendered meaningless. Perhaps this explains, to some extent, the approach adopted by French artist Pierre Huyghe in the extraordinarily ambitious installation at the Kunsthaus Bregenz, *L'expédition scintillante*. Recognizing that our relationship to such places can only ever be abstract, Huyghe adopted fiction rather than a misplaced documentary realism as the most appropriate form of engagement, creating a series of works on each floor of the gallery. In perhaps the most striking display, the floor of the large square space was clad entirely in raw pine, while mist, rain and even snow fell from openings in the ceiling. A light bounced around the ceiling grid; a shortwave radio seemed to move between static voices and sound (in fact, it was a piece by American composer John Cage); and there, in the centre of the space, a boat made entirely of ice melted slowly away. On the level above, two white boxes were placed in the centre of the empty space, one on the floor and the other a few feet above it; between them smoke curled, illuminated by an ever-changing pattern of coloured lights, while Claude Debussy's orchestration of Erik Satie's *Gymnopédies* floated from the structure, as if some form of post-impressionist synaesthesia. On the top floor, a large poster showed a polar landscape with scribbled black-and-white lines upon which white text declared: 'L'expédition scintillante – a musical'. Long black leather benches lined the edges of the room, while in the centre, a low black form is revealed, upon closer inspection, to be a polished ice rink, the traces of the skater still visible upon its surface. An accompanying publication makes reference to fictional travels of old – Poe's Arthur Gordon Pym or the sequel by Jules Verne – the three acts in the book referring to the three floors of the installation, the passage from journey, to experience, to a representation of that experience. Yet the work is no documentary record of a journey that has taken place, but rather a scenario for a collective expedition yet to come, a poetic expedition rather than a scientific one, and one that can be joined by anyone at any point.

'O my God! What sublime scenery I have beheld.... The Mist broke in the middle; and at last stood as the waters of the Red Sea are said to have done when the Israelites passed – & between the two walls of Mist the Sunlight *burnt* upon the Ice a strait *Road* of golden Fire, all across the lake – intolerably bright, & the walls of Mist partaking of the light in a multitude of colours. – About a month ago the vehemence of the wind had shattered the Ice – part of it, quite smattered, was driven to shore & had frozen anew; this was of a deep blue & represented an agitated sea – the water, that ran up between the great Islands of Ice, shone of a yellow green (it was at sunset) and all the scattered islands of *smooth* ice were *blood*; intensely bright *Blood*: on some of the largest Islands the Fishermen were pulling out their immense nets thro' the Holes made in the Ice for this purpose, & the Fishermen, the net poles, & the huge nets made a part of the Glory!'

Samuel Taylor Coleridge, in a 1799 letter to his wife describing ice-skating in Germany

L'expédition scintillante, Act 1, Untitled (ice boat)
Pierre Huyghe, 2002

In 1975, at the age of nineteen, the American artist Roni Horn made her first trip abroad. She chose Iceland as her destination. Since then, she has travelled to the country once, sometimes twice, a year, every year. As she has noted, referring to a five-month visit in 1979, during which time she had spent most of her time camping and travelling by motorcycle: 'The scale of the island made an enormous impression on me. It is big enough to get lost on, but small enough to find oneself.' This sense of a spiritual journey is central to Horn's ongoing response to this extraordinary place. On the rear endpapers of her book *To Place – Book I: Bluff Life* (1990), Horn quotes Simone Weil's desire in *Gravity and Grace*, 'To see a landscape as it is when I'm not there.' It is a beautiful thought, though as Horn readily acknowledges, 'such a desire can only be thwarted'. Yet a desire thwarted is not a desire negated but a desire intensified, and rather than allowing this to prevent her from making work, Horn uses it, instead, to enable her. In stating that 'the view is not separate from the viewer', Horn recognizes one of the most important relationships in an understanding of place within contemporary art: a desire to re-enchant the land with meaning, or to examine that area of overlap and coincidence between inner and outer spaces.

This relationship between inner and outer, between the body and its surroundings, has been explored by Horn in a number of works, including *Becoming a Landscape*. The work consists of a number of paired photographs, six pairs of close-up views of thermal springs, and three pairs of portraits of the same young person. Interestingly, it is the portraits that are most difficult to read: the young face, framed above jacket and below knitted hat, carries an expression of perfectly inscrutability; more than this, even the subject's age and gender is indeterminate. On the contrary, the images of the geysers seem almost palpably corporeal, wet openings that act as thresholds between interior and exterior spaces. The threshold is also explored in another of Horn's photographic works, *Her, Her, Her, and Her*, which consists of a grid of black-and-white photographs taken in the changing rooms of the Sundhöllin í Reykjavík indoor swimming pool, built between 1929 and 1937 and a favourite of the artist. Here the clean, calibrated, tile-gridded spaces of the rooms and corridors contrast with the blurred figures visible through the small circular windows on the changing-room doors, a pure geometric form opening up intimately onto the bodily spaces that are glimpsed fleetingly within.

'My image of Iceland as a reflecting pool is the idea of using nature as mirror and measure. It's an understanding of oneself through a knowledge of what real, not imposed, limitations are. My experiences in the ice-and-ash desert interior of Iceland provided an especially accurate reflection. The desert is a mirror. It's a self-contained environment. It gives nothing. What you take from the desert is who you are, more precisely.... Inner geography is a plain knowledge of oneself, a kind of common sense gathered through repeated exposure to distilling experiences. Inner geography maps peace of mind in the world as it is and not as I imagine it.'

Roni Horn

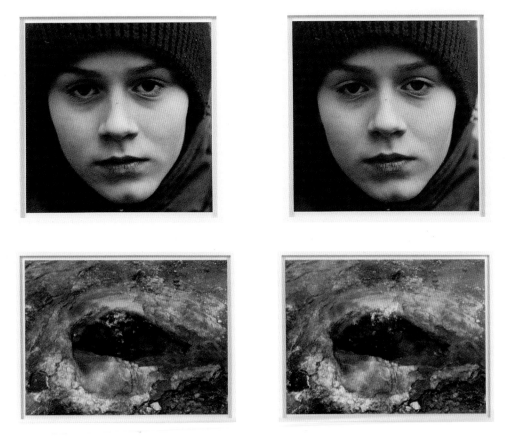

'Iceland is primarily young geology. Young geology is very unstable. In a literal sense, Iceland is not a very stable place. Iceland is always becoming what it will be, and what it will be is not a fixed thing either. So here is Iceland: an act, not an object, a verb, never a noun. Iceland taught me that each place is a unique location of change. No place is a fixed or concluded thing. So I have discarded the noun form of place as meaningless.'

Roni Horn

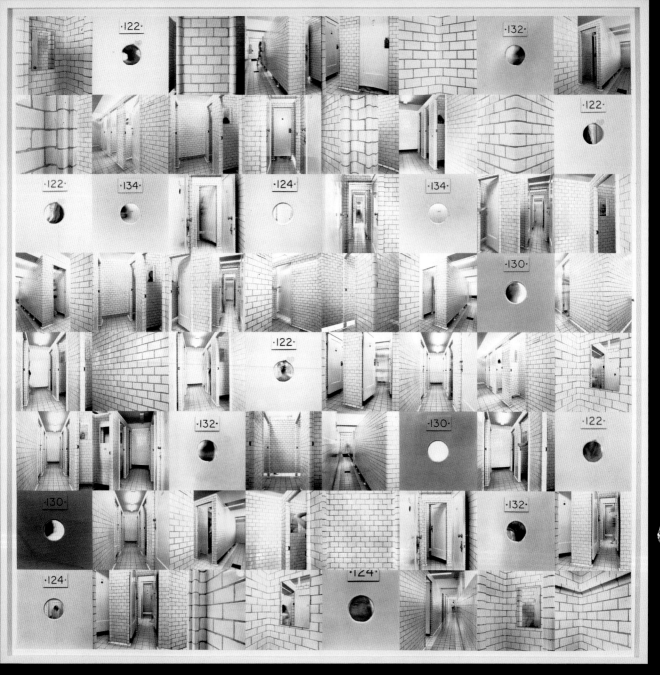

Her, Her, Her, and Her (2)
Roni Horn, 2002

FANTASTIC

As with our ideas of the city and of nature, place in its many forms fires the imagination. Our minds can easily take us on flights of fancy to faraway and unreal places. But these places need not be unusual or unfamiliar. Perhaps their fantastic nature is revealed even more when we know the location intimately but suddenly become aware of its strange and uncanny character. Even supposed alien encounters must occur in a place that is local to someone, in their everyday.

'Shot simultaneously in London and Iceland, September 2001

A remote viewer is a person trained to focus and hold his or her subconscious mind on a distant target that is normally shielded by time and space and record information about that distant person, place or event.

The artist made a trip to Askja in Iceland and during this time a remote viewer attempted to trace/locate the artist without having any prior knowledge of the subject or his whereabouts.

The central issues here are those of projection and reception and in a way these elements become interchangeable. The remote viewer seems to invent or project the landscape rather than perceive it and the landscape seems to sense his presence. The use of the infinity screen as the projection wall for the landscape footage completes this inversion as it is the background on which the remote viewer was filmed. It seems to catch the image as it is thrown up by the remote viewer. The two screens face each other and so constantly refer to this mental loop as the viewer switches from one to the other.'

Graham Gussin

Adam Chodzko's work is often concerned with the description of place, and the rituals that might make up that description. In *Involva* (1995), a pencil drawing of a forest was reproduced in a sex contact magazine along with the (we are assured) genuine enquiry: 'Please will you join me here?' We are left to imagine where 'here' actually is, and what might possibly take place there. In other works, the location is made more explicit, such as in *A Place for The End* (1999), where eight residents of Birmingham were each invited to select somewhere that could be used as the location for the final shot of an imaginary film, fantasy here being projected onto even familiar surroundings. If such pieces suggest other places, then this is especially true of *Better Scenery*, a series of works each consisting of two large signs upon which is written the directions to the other sign, thereby inviting the viewer to imagine not only the other location, but also how the place in which he or she now finds themselves might also be described.

Better Scenery (Detail: Arizona Desert, USA;
Sainsbury's car park, Finchley Road, London, UK)
Adam Chodzko, 2001

Better Scenery (Detail: Grizedale Forest, Cumbria, UK; Italdesign factory, Turin, Italy)
Adam Chodzko, 2001

Better Scenery (Detail: Angel Mews, Islington, London, UK; Fargo, North Dakota, USA)
Adam Chodzko, 2002

In 1985, the then sixteen-year-old German artist Gregor Schneider moved into a vacant apartment on the grounds of his father's lead foundry in Rheydt and began a process of continual alteration to the building that continues to this day. The *Totes Haus ur* (Dead House ur) is a strange, labyrinthine space that exists behind a tiled three-storey façade, an insistent architectural reminder that Freud's uncanny, the *unheimlich*, is closely related to the homely, or *heimlich*. Here, walls are built in front of other identical walls, thereby rendering the changes perceptible, but unrecognizable. Often the new walls and floors are lined with a thick sound-insulating material such as lead, thereby altering the rooms' characteristics in other invisible ways, the increasingly oppressive atmosphere palpable nonetheless. Windows are built in front of other windows, lamps placed in the spaces between them so that natural light appears to flood through the net curtains even when it is dark outside. The entrances to rooms are hidden behind walls, while even more familiar doors create anxiety, the handles often loose, or unable to be manipulated from the inside of a closed room. It is a building of intense spatial and temporal dislocation, and one that seems to suggest a moral one too. Yet while the rooms may remind us of those found in horror movies, or repulsive news reports, we should be wary of characterizing them as evidence of – indeed, scenes of – some form of psycho-sexual drama, a response which Schneider's reluctance to explain his motives no doubt encourages. Instead, perhaps this extraordinary project could be considered a form of exploration of a greater collective memory, of communities lost – such as those displaced by the large-scale strip-mining nearby – and of places haunted by those who once belonged there.

'The law of the fantastic condemns it to encounter instruments only. These instruments are not…meant to serve men, but rather to manifest unremittingly an evasive, preposterous finality. This accounts for the labyrinth of corridors, doors and staircases that lead to nothing, the signposts that lead to nothing, the innumerable signs that line the road and that mean nothing. In the "topsy-turvy" world, the means are isolated and posed for their own sake.'
Jean-Paul Sartre

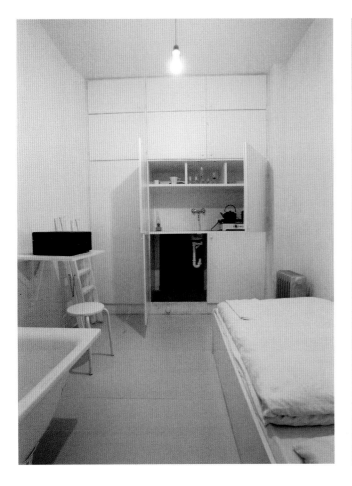

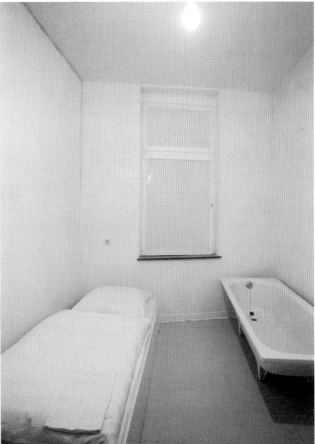

Totes Haus ur
Gregor Schneider, 2001

Totes Haus ur
Gregor Schneider, 2001

'From the idea of "homelike", belonging to the house, the further idea is developed of something withdrawn from the eyes of strangers, something concealed, secret.... "Heimlich" is used in conjunction with a verb expressing the act of concealing....

Officials who give important advice which has to be kept secret in matters of state are called *heimlich* councillors; the adjective, according to modern usage, has been replaced by *geheim* [secret]....

Heimlich, as used of knowledge – mystic, allegorical: a *heimlich* meaning, *mysticus, divinus, occultus, figuratus*. *Heimlich* in a different sense, as withdrawn from knowledge, unconscious.... *Heimlich* also has the meaning of that which is obscure, inaccessible to knowledge.

The notion of something hidden and dangerous...is still further developed, so that "heimlich" comes to have the meaning usually ascribed to "unheimlich". Thus: "At times I feel like a man who walks in the night and believes in ghosts; every corner is *heimlich* and full of terrors for him." '

Jacob and Wilhelm Grimm

'Some people look at them and think they look throw-away, trashy and about nothing, other people might find them scary and frightening. If we look at the paintings with the polluted lakes, the Disney Nuclear Power Station and the mutant bugs, on one level they are about the environment and the arrogance of human beings who have created this world, [and] part of me would like to make incredibly dry, serious work about those issues, but on the other hand I want there to be some pleasure and humour in the storytelling.'

Liz Arnold

Liz Arnold's paintings have been described as being as much about inventing a world as they are about the invention of worlds. Certainly, she paints the white-coated scientists of our media-saturated imagination, standing awe-struck – horrified and exhilarated – before their miscreant creations in anonymous laboratory interiors, or in the strangely illuminated landscapes on whose threshold they stand, and perhaps we could view the artist in a similar manner. There is an enjoyment to be had in viewing the work, but it is an uneasy pleasure, as we attempt to comprehend what is going on in these unusual places of flat shapes and sour colours. Often the places are superficially attractive, such as mountainside lakes or beaches, or tropical islands, perhaps caught in the glow of an idealized sunset, yet we seldom feel that these are places for us. Perhaps it is their lack of illusionistic depth that prevents us from entering into them; more likely is the very unnaturalness of the scenes themselves, the colours seeming as viewed through a filter, or under UV light, thereby creating works in which the exotic is reconfigured into the toxic.

'That an island is deserted must appear *philosophically* normal to us. Humans cannot live, nor live in security, unless they assume that the active struggle between earth and water is over, or at least contained…. Humans can live on an island only by forgetting what an island represents. Islands are either from before or for after humankind.'

Gilles Deleuze

top
Melt
Liz Arnold, 2000

bottom
Island
Liz Arnold, 1999

Long Distance
Liz Arnold, 2000

opposite
Brunettes
Liz Arnold, 2000

New Manhattan City 3021
Bodys Isek Kingelez, 2001–2

The Congolese artist Bodys Isek Kingelez creates highly coloured models of buildings and, indeed, entire cityscapes from simple materials such as plywood and cardboard, although their sheer exuberance exceeds these humble beginnings. In *Ville Fantôme* (1996), glass-and-steel buildings, reminiscent of those that emerged from the Bauhaus are found alongside towering mirrored columns more familiar from mid-twentieth-century 'visions of the future' than from our own cities. One building has a sign near its top which proclaims: 'USA'; another reads 'Seoul'. It is a city that emerges from a particular vision of progress, and the same is true of *New Manhattan City 3021*, a vision of lower Manhattan as it might appear in the next millennium, a vision obviously marked by the discussions surrounding its redevelopment following the destruction of 11 September 2001. Like much of Kingelez's work, it is much influenced by past visions of the future, whether it be the futurism of the Italian architect Antonio Sant'Elia or the consumer utopianism of postwar American cartoons, the city as a candy-coloured playground, the shape of things to come. Whether one sees these places as desirable or not – and therefore whether one sees the work as critical or not – obviously depends on from where one views the work; one can only imagine how these places might be seen by an inhabitant of the Democratic Republic of the Congo, one of the most war-ravaged countries on Earth. Our sense of any other place is very much dependent upon the sense that we have of our own.

'The future of America is the future of the world. Material circumstances are driving all nations along the path in which America is going. Living in the contemporary environment, which is everywhere becoming more and more American, men feel a psychological compulsion to go the American way. Fate acts within and without; there is no resisting. For good or for evil, it seems the world must be Americanised. America is not unique; she merely leads the way along the road which the people of every nation and continent are taking. Studying the good and the evil features of American life, we are studying, in a generally more definite and highly developed form, the good and evil features of the whole world's present and immediately coming civilisation. Speculating on the American future, we are speculating on the future of civilised man.'

Aldous Huxley

Since 1995, the British artist Paul Noble has been
working on a series of large-scale drawings – and,
most recently, an animated film – of an imaginary,
unpopulated metropolis called 'Nobson Newtown',
a place which, as its name suggests, combines
personal idiosyncrasy with an attempted rationality.
Often awkwardly rendered in graphite pencil – Noble's
motto is the rather ignoble 'No style, no technique,
no accidents, only mistakes' – the work is the dark
antithesis to the playful autocracy of computer games
such as *Sim City*, a dark satire upon our construction of
the modern world and our neo-romantic superimposition
of identity and environment. It is, as the artist describes
it, 'town planning as self-portraiture' by way of
explaining his place as the only inhabitant.

'Nor could I ever after see the world as I
had known it. Mixed with the present scene
was always a little of the past and a little of
the future, and every once-familiar object
loomed alien in the new perspective brought
on by my widened sight. From then on I
walked in a fantastic dream of unknown
and half-known shapes; and with each
new gateway crossed, the less plainly could
I recognize the things of the narrow sphere
to which I had so long been bound.'
H. P. Lovecraft

Unified Nobson
Paul Noble, 2001

Silbury Hill
25 July 1997

Crop Circle Geometry and Construction Lines

by Bert Janssen

In 1998 two crop circles with seven-fold geometry appeared quite close to each other. The first one appeared in the East Field of Alton Barnes and the second one near Tawsmead Copse. Their appearance showed many similarities.

The following geometrical analysis will illustrate that not only did they show many similarities, they were also very strongly related to each other. The two formations are like brother and sister, they have the same geometrical genes so to speak. Furthermore I will show you that the construction lines found in both formations will turn out to be of unexpected value! But let us first take a closer look at the Tawsmead Copse formation.

Note: all diagrams came into being by means of construction, that is, without measuring anything.

(I will show you in a future article how seven-fold geometry can be constructed. For now, please consider it true that indeed it can be done...)

In Diagram 1 a seven-fold star was constructed. Within that star, a circle and a heptahedron can be constructed. This was done in Diagram 2.

Furthermore, as you can see in Diagram 3, another seven-fold star can be constructed within the star of Diagram 1.

Diagram 1

Diagram 2

continued on page 16

15

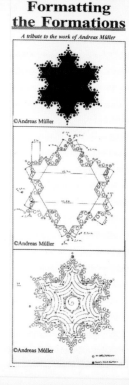

©Andreas Müller

©Andreas Müller

©Andreas Müller

Since 1991, British artist Rod Dickinson has been making crop circles with friends and other artists, working at night with simple materials – a surveyor's tape measure, wooden boards, and rope – to produce increasingly complex patterns in the cereal fields of southern England. Most crop circle researchers – or cerealogists – believe the patterns to be produced by extra-terrestrial or paranormal forces, a belief no doubt suggested by the fact that most of the major patterns are found in Wiltshire, traditionally the home of English paganism and New Age mythology, and the site of numerous ancient earthworks, such as Silbury Hill and Stonehenge, as well as the Alton Barnes White Horse, cut into a hillside. The mythology of such a place – of a landscape marked with ley lines or energy centres – enables Dickinson's creations to enter a mutually dependent value system between cerealogist and artist,

even if the former denies the responsibility of the latter in their search for an explanation that moves beyond human activity to an occult relationship between the land and unknown and perhaps unknowable forces. It is certainly true that the adoption, more recently, of crop circles within advertising and the manufacture of large-scale designs to promote corporate brands does represent a form of supra-individual power, albeit one wedded to capital rather than the occult.

above

Diagrams and cuttings taken from crop circle researchers' and enthusiasts' pamphlets
Rod Dickinson, 1997

opposite

Crop Formation, Silbury Hill, Wiltshire
Rod Dickinson, 1997

Crop Formation, Woodborough Hill, Wiltshire
Rod Dickinson, 2000

MYTH / HISTORY

Often our everyday, ordinary places have been witness to extraordinary events. These may be significant enough to have been recorded in the annals of history, or perhaps they are the less consequential – but no less significant – moments of daily life, the memories of which have been passed down the generations. These are places traversed as much by stories as by footsteps. Sometimes they take their identity from their myths; at other times, the myths emerge from the place itself; at yet others, the place and its history are at odds with each other, although each helps create the other.

top
Handball Alleys, St Enda's College,
Galway, Ireland
Dorothy Cross, 1999

bottom
Poll na bPéist (The Worm's Hole), Inis
Mór, Aran Islands, Co. Galway, Ireland
Dorothy Cross, 1999

'There are more than 370 handball alleys scattered around Ireland. Largely disused, they stand like modernist sculptures: beautiful, empty arenas. Poll na bPéist (The Worm's Hole) is located on the terraced cliffs at the back of Inis Mór, the Aran Islands. The exquisite rectangular pool is fed subterraneanly by the ocean. It rises and falls with the tides and weather. A natural structure, it was formed geologically. The proportions of the pool mirror those of the handball alleys.

The film, projected from two 90-foot towers, fills the floor of the alleys. The film, doubled, meets the dividing wall, producing kaleidoscopic Rorschachs. They overlap the geometry of the moving rectangle of water with the still alleys. I selected the fragments of song from ten romantic operas; famous stories of love and loss, and extremes of passion. For *Chiasm* the voices are divorced from the orchestral music. The alley wall separates the tenor from the soprano. The singers move within the same projections. The roles shift from Romeo to Ariadne, Dido to Desdemona, Othello to Manon…. The narrative is broken and the characters confused. Like a string of pearls, duets occur and disappear.'
Dorothy Cross

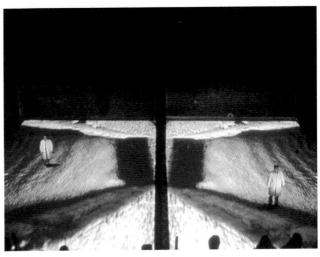

Stills from Chiasm
Dorothy Cross, 1999

The Spanish-born and London-based artist Juan Cruz is fascinated by stories, how they are told as much as what it is they tell (to some extent, stories only exist in their telling). This was apparent in his first major work, *Translating Don Quijote* (1996), performed, appropriately, in London's Instituto Cervantes, where the artist spoke his own translation of the great work over a series of three-hour periods, thereby reanimating it in a manner reminiscent of – but importantly different from – the eponymous protagonist of Borges's extraordinary short story 'Pierre Menard, author of *Don Quixote*'. In *Sancti Petri* (1998) the artist presents us with descriptions of the abandoned Spanish town, both visual and verbal. A series of slides projected upon a free-standing screen shows in a clear and methodical manner the buildings, roads and their crossings, of this former fish-canning town; Cruz's careful narration leads us through the streets too, encouraging us to investigate the place further. And yet for all the clarity of these two means, their simplicity, their transparency, we are left uncertain. Sancti Petri remains a place both real and imagined.

Cruz played with the conventions of fact and fiction, information and imagination, yet further in his work for the Melbourne Festival 2001. Like many artists invited to participate in international festivals and biennials, Cruz had not visited the city previously, and so felt uncomfortable in making a site-specific work with little understanding of its location, culture or complexities. However, he chose to acknowledge this situation, and use it as the basis for a piece in which imagination and local understanding come together in subtle but inextricable ways. For *Application for Planning Permit: Proposal to Build a Metaphor* (2001), Cruz adopted one of the formal means of describing urban space, the 'Notice of Application for Planning Permit', as the basis for a series of public works situated at twelve locations around Melbourne. At each location – each well known or remarkable in some way, such as the Old Magistrates Court, the Sidney Meyer Music Bowl, or Flinders Street Station, from which Australia's first train ran in 1854 – was placed an A1-sized permit poster as specified by local planning regulations. However, instead of details of a new commercial development, in addition to the standard bureaucratic information the posters contained a short piece of writing by Cruz, each highlighting a different aspect of life within a small Castilian village, and each relating to the location in which they were placed. And so, outside the State Library of Victoria we read of a young man and the circumstances that led him to study art history, a decision which, in turn, influenced his choice of books to read during his summer holidays as he sat outside the refuge he maintained at the top of a hill overlooking the village. The posters at the Sandridge Railway Bridge told of the river-crabs that were a rare local delicacy before being wiped out in a misguided attempt at farming them. The river was later restocked with a more resilient Californian variety, the crayfish, and the river-crab became an even greater part of local folklore, a large bronze statue of one being erected on the outskirts of the village along the river, and a new feast day being established in their honour. In its own way, it is a fable of how the inhabitants of a place can destroy that which makes its everyday experience unique, necessitating both its replacement by a less specific global culture, and its further transformation into myth, an exaggerated sense of identity appreciated more by tourists, one suspects, than the inhabitants themselves.

'Cruz's choice affords a local viewer a snapshot of how we present ourselves to the world beyond: the weight we place on certain cultural sites and locations and the images this then presents to outsiders. However, on reading Cruz's narratives further – and possibly expecting greater enlightenment as to the significant aspects of our city through the eyes of an outsider – the reader is presented with a series of stories about a place and people unknown to the viewer, but familiar in shared social experiences. Thus Cruz's choice and descriptions of sites in a city yet unseen by him bring the viewer full-circle, by presenting images to the reader of yet another unknown, unexperienced, and unseen.'

Rebecca Coates

João Penalva's video work *336 PEK* (336 Rivers) shares many of the characteristics of the rest of his oeuvre – a certain visual enticement, the presence of forms of human communication, the uncertainties of translation, and the perpetual instability of meaning. In a cinema-like space within the gallery is projected a luminous image, a landscape view, which has had its colours altered; the row of trees halfway up the projection, which screen from our view the distant beyond, are a dark green, as are the shadows upon the grass cast by two more trees in the midground, yet the rest of the view is an acidic yellow, with a bright white burning along the edges of the branches or the shimmering line below the arboreal backdrop. The image bristles, as if with static, and yet appears relatively static itself, unchanging, we suspect, until we notice the strange spectral presence of people crossing the open space, a woman walking her dog, for example, or the breeze. And over the scene is the hypnotic sound of a Russian voice, the actor Yuri Stepanov, as he relates to us stories, stories that possess a sense of being familiar, as though passed down through families or exchanged between people while shopping or read in local newspapers, stories about which we can never be certain, however, even when we see them before us, fixed in white as subtitles upon the screen.

The 336 rivers of the title run into what, for Penalva, is the main character of the film: not the nameless narrator, but Lake Baikal, 'a lake 550 kilometres long and 44 kilometres wide. This vastness, this amount of fresh water looming in the background is not easy to imagine, it is not in the background of the image, and it can only be, in some way or other, in the mind. Once this happens, anything is possible.' The lake becomes an accumulation of folklore and myth, fed by cultural tributaries: according to one mythic tale, it is where the 'locomotive of Prince Kilkhov' lies, on its bed; according to another, the train has been raised to the surface to run, once more, between Helsinki and St Petersburg.

Two different versions of the swan maiden's story exist also, the legend that gives the lake its name. We even learn that there are more than 336 rivers leading into the lake, 460 we are told (and how are we to know?), although only 277 have names. It is difficult to imagine a river without a name, but because there is so much to imagine here, this concerns us little. As Stepanov recites the names of the rivers that have them, we hear their waters burbling in his voice, flowing around vowels and crashing against consonants, and we are left with our memories of a place we do not know.

'The section of the rivers' names is… an aural experience, but it is an aural experience inside another aural experience – a much easier one to bear, as it follows a narrative pattern of linked stories, both personal and folkloric, in a language not widely understood but melodic and attractive in its foreignness…. If people doze off in the "rivers section" they will be on the shores of the Baikal, they will hear its waves.'

João Penalva

336 PEK (336 Rivers)
João Penalva, 1998

The Danish artist Joachim Koester often uses the mode of documentary – and, in particular, the medium of photography – in order to dramatize the history of a particular place. Sometimes the dramatization is made explicit: in *Day for Night, Christiania* (1996) Koester photographed the self-proclaimed autonomous territory established in the 1960s on the site of a seventeenth-century military base in the heart of Copenhagen, and now threatened with closure – or at least tighter regulation – by the Danish authorities. Using a blue filter that produces the 'day-for-night' effect familiar from Hollywood films – '*la nuit américaine*', as the French call it – Koester reveals the workings of the fantastic upon the actual, just as the dual titles of the works – *The Milkyway/Officers' Quarters*, for example – make clear the layering of a utopian future upon a militaristic past. More often the dramatization is less apparent. In *Row Housing* (2002), for example, Koester photographed the isolated town of Resolute on Cornwallis Island, in the Canadian Arctic, in the Inuit State of Nunavut. It is a place of a devastating beauty that possesses a history of devastation. Sir John Franklin sailed around the island during his disastrous 1845 expedition to find the North-West Passage; just over one hundred years later, Inuit families were brought here from their homes over a thousand miles away, in an act of 'rehabilitation', a misguided attempt to situate people in an environment in which they did not belong. The effects upon the population were predictably appalling, although these are not immediately apparent in Koester's compassionately distant gaze. Nevertheless, we are reminded, in the words of Robert Smithson (an important artist for Koester) that each landscape, no matter how calm and lovely, conceals a substratum of disaster.

This is no doubt also true of the landscapes of the Bialowieza Forest, which is situated on the border of central and eastern Europe and dates back to 8000 BC and is the only remaining example of the primeval lowland forest that once covered much of Europe. Famous for centuries as the home of the European bison, through the years it has been a place that exists in the realm of mythology as much as geography, as a Sylvan arcadia, an asylum, or a pristine Eden, a sacred grove and a dark and alien impenetrable wilderness. Poles, Lithuanians, Germans and Russians have mapped the forest as a homeland, a setting for national identity, utilizing its distinctiveness to illuminate national character – the Reichsmarschall Hermann Goering even saw the German occupation of the area in 1939 as an opportunity to welcome back what he believed was a pure 'Teutonic Ur-wald' long vanished from German soil. Such are the myths that grow from and upon this rich earth.

'This was the order of human institutions: first the forests, after that the huts, then the villages, next the cities, and finally the academies.'
Giambattista Vico

Bialowieza Forest
Joachim Koester, 2001

'Topical History:
Places remember events'
James Joyce

'It might be a parody, but it's also a tribute. It's like freezing the moment in which truth turns into hallucination. There is something hypnotic in Hollywood: it's a sign that immediately speaks about obsessions, failures and ambitions. It is a magnet for contradictions.'

Maurizio Cattelan

It is a continuing irony that the place that presents the world with the most spectacular of images can only offer the most rudimentary image of itself, a sign on a hillside that announces its location – HOLLYWOOD. Standing high upon the Hollywood Hills, the nine letters also stand for what we understand about the place – a place for dreams, illusions and ambition, and the darker attributes that lurk in the shadows thrown by all that sparkles there. For the 2001 Venice Biennale, Maurizio Cattelan built a replica of the sign, 170 metres wide, which was then placed on Bellolampo hill in Palermo, above the city dump. As Cattelan remarked, 'It's like spraying stardust over the Sicilian landscape.... I tried to overlap two opposite realities, Sicily and Hollywood: after all, images are just projections of desire, and I wanted to shade their boundary.' The placing of a sign of imaginary escape overlooking a landscape made of the detritus of everyday life is a telling conjunction, perhaps even an act of transgression between myth and reality. Such an act is not one of simple opposition but, as French philosopher Michel Foucault has written of difference in 'Preface to Transgression': 'Perhaps it is like a flash of lightning in the night which, from the beginning of time, gives a dense and black intensity to the night which it denies, which lights up the night from the inside, from top to bottom, and yet owes to the dark the stark clarity of its manifestation, its harrowing and poised singularity.' It is this relationship that is played out above Palermo, on a hillside called Bellolampo, 'a beautiful flash of lightning'.

Hollywood
Maurizio Cattelan, 2001

'Re-creating the myth of Hollywood in Sicily, Cattelan displaces
multiple meanings, through the use of few, gigantic letters.'
Harald Szeemann

'Parallel narratives are evoked, mapping one history over another as the material presence of the text literally goes up in smoke.

Here an ephemeral and transient gesture is recorded as a mark of respect in an ongoing process of dislocation and relocation.

"Just another elapsure of time, designated."'

Cerith Wyn Evans

For his film *Firework Text (Pasolini)*, British artist Cerith Wyn Evans built a firework-and-wood construction – itself called *P.P.P. (Oedipus Rex)* – on an Italian beach that displayed 'quotations' from poet and film-maker Pier Paolo Pasolini's *Oedipus Rex* (1967): 'On the banks of the Livenza / silvery willows are growing / in wild profusion, their boughs / dipping into the drifting waters.' These lines describe the landscape Pasolini knew as a child, and which he recalled many years later as an adult in his films. In Wyn Evans's presentation of them, however, Pasolini's 'memories' last only a few moments, until they go up in flames, letter by letter, and, in the flash of an explosion, finally disappear into the darkness of the night.

Firework Text (Pasolini)
Cerith Wyn Evans, 1998

The sociologist John Urry has written that: 'Like the pilgrim the tourist moves from a familiar place to a far place and then returns to the familiar place. At the far place both the pilgrim and the tourist engage in "worship" of shrines which are sacred, albeit in different ways, and as a result gain some kind of uplifting experience.' It is such a journey we must consider with Rodney Graham's recent work *Aberdeen*, a tribute to the rock star Kurt Cobain, charismatic frontman of Nirvana, although how sacred the shrines, and how uplifting the resultant experience, remains open to question. Graham, the fan, travelled from his native Vancouver across the border into Washington state and to the dreary backwater of Aberdeen, the despised birthplace of Cobain, where he took a number of photographs which he then projected from a slide carousel. While historic shrines are often in a state of decay, here the dereliction is less ancient than modern, abandoned warehouses or factory units, and the objects of veneration are not finely handcrafted from precious materials but instead gaudily mass-produced.

Another sociologist, Erik Cohen, has proposed that pilgrimage is defined by a movement from the 'profane periphery' to the 'sacred centre', while tourism, by contrast, involves a movement from the cultural centre to the periphery, or to the centre of other cultures and societies. Graham's journey seems to consist of both movements simultaneously, a movement between places that remain both centres and peripheries, depending upon the place from which they are considered.

this page and opposite
Aberdeen
Rodney Graham, 2000

'*08/05 (Kinloch Rannoch) 13/08* (2002–2020) aims to encompass the epicentral position of Rannoch Moor within the Marises' work. This vast project utilizes a variety of archival media including text, photography, binaural recording, film and digital video, to develop a series of deconstructions based upon the historical documentation of Joseph Beuys's two seminal journeys to the moor.

The first journey, on the 8th of May 1970, during which Beuys collected the materials for *The Loch Awe Piece*, was captured on two rolls of Kodak TRI-X film by Richard Demarco and Sally Holman. Careful study of the Demarco negatives has enabled the Marises to reconstruct the original route and establish precise locations for their re-photographic deconstruction entitled *08/05*.

The second journey, which was poignantly documented in the film *Joseph Beuys in Scotland* by Rory McEwen, took place on the 13th of August 1970, and marks the overture to Beuys's *Celtic (Kinloch Rannoch) Scottish Symphony*.

In August 2002 the Marises reshot the McEwen film scene for scene, diligently replicating each camera movement and plane of focus, as if to highlight the palpable absence of Joseph Beuys.'

Alexander and Susan Maris

Luc Tuymans's paintings often seem like the thickened shadows of memory that have stained the canvases across which they have been cast. His extraordinary body of work *Mwana Kitoko* (2000), which was first exhibited in the Belgian Pavilion at the 2001 Venice Biennale, explores his country's colonial relationship with what was known as the Belgian Congo. The title is taken from a rather derogatory nickname given to the twenty-four-year-old Belgian king Badouin I by the Congolese during his first visit to the colony in 1955, the 'beautiful boy' who is seen in one painting in gleaming white uniform and peaked cap disembarking from an aeroplane. Another portrait in the series, *Lumumba*, shows the first democratically elected Prime Minister of the independent Democratic Republic of the Congo (later Zaire), Patrice Lumumba, who came to power in 1960, a year before being brutally murdered in an attack that has been linked to both the Belgian government and the CIA. These paintings, like Tuymans's representations of Independence Day celebrations in 1960 or the symbols of state and religious power, such as *The Mission*, refuse to make explicit any reading of the tragic events that make up the late colonial history of his native country, but rather turn their attention towards incidental details or events that suggest the violence and corruption of power that clearly took place. For Tuymans, these are places connected by history, places that are created by history, a history that he reveals as a complex web of memories that may be partial, blurred or faded.

'In spite of the dominant presence of the building in the landscape, this painting shows us a constructed reality that was fictional from the start. The mission station is a fragment of a larger spatial project, in which it was to form the locus of a new imported memory.... *The Mission* is based on the idea of an abandoned and unfinished project. It is an after-image of the colonial fact, of a modern way of "being" in the world. In a vast landscape, underneath a loaded sky, literally "in the middle of nowhere", the typical colonial mission station stands as an idiolect: alien, massive, and turned in on itself. The cross mutilates the space by its dramatic position, but it is unable to command a presence so close to the building. The painting clearly shows the degree to which such a building is an addition that is forced upon an existing physical space.'

Philippe Pirotte

'What gives place its specificity is not some long internalized history but the fact that it is constructed out of a particular constellation of social relations, meeting and weaving together at a particular locus.... Instead then, of thinking of places as areas with boundaries around them, they can be imagined as articulated moments in networks of social relations and understandings, but where a large proportion of those relations, experiences and understandings are constructed on a far larger scale than what we happen to define for that moment as the place itself, whether it be a street, or a region or even a continent. And this in turn allows a sense of place which is extroverted, which includes a consciousness of its links with the wider world, which integrates in a positive way the global and the local.'

Doreen Massey

POLITICS / CONTROL

Place is always political. Even to keep a place empty, in a 'natural state', is a political act. The myths of a place are often maintained, or resurrected, for political purposes, perhaps as a prelude to a territorial claim or to the expulsion of groups deemed to be 'out of place'. Sometimes a sense of place emerges from the 'ground up', from the ties that bind a community, although these can often be cut by the workings of national or global politics. Sometimes it is useful, politically, to create a new place and try to build communities or to engender a new sense of belonging. To develop a place, or to save it, is to act politically, often upon the foundations of myth and history.

In 1984, the British National Coal Board proposed a series of pit closures; without balloting its members, the National Union of Mineworkers went on strike in protest at the closures. The dispute, which lasted for over a year, was the most bitterly fought since the general strike of 1926 and its effects upon the British economy – and society – were far-reaching and continue to be felt to this day. It was on 8 June 1984 that one of the most shocking incidents of the dispute occurred, near the Orgreave Coking Plant in South Yorkshire: a violent confrontation between striking miners and ranks of police, which led to a cavalry charge through the village. It is this confrontation that Jeremy Deller re-enacted in his work *The Battle of Orgreave*, in collaboration with Howard Giles, an expert in historical re-enactment, and using members of historical re-enactment societies from all over Britain, as well as people local to Orgreave, some of whom were involved in the original confrontation.

In some ways there were a number of layers to the original dispute: the recurring battle between the Conservative government and the NUM (which had brought down a Conservative administration a decade earlier), which became a battle of wills between their respective leaders, Margaret Thatcher and Arthur Scargill, was certainly one. But it was also a battle between the global flow of capital and the situatedness of communities. Towns that had become established, historically, because of the fates of geology and their proximity to accessible raw materials were now threatened by the burgeoning international trade in commodities such as coal, a globalization that had developed from the Industrial Revolution that these very towns had helped power. It was not simply jobs that were being fought for here, but also local identity and the importance of place to our continued sense of self.

Deller's re-enactment brought all of these issues, still raw in the town's collective memory, into the present. The work highlighted the fact that the original dispute, which had torn the local community apart, pitting neighbour against neighbour, brother against brother, depending on which side of the dividing line they found themselves, remains alive to this day, as many of the divisions from 1984 still linger. But at the same time, the re-enactment had a tragic, nostalgic aspect, for it revealed the extent to which the original battle had been in vain, as the march of global capitalism continues regardless.

'Every event described in history, every series of events reconstructed, has to have a place.'
F. Lukermann

The Battle of Orgreave
Jeremy Deller, 2001

'Once knowledge can be analysed in terms of region, domain, implantation, displacement, transposition, one is able to capture the process by which knowledge functions as a form of power and disseminates the effects of power.'

Michel Foucault

German photographer Thomas Demand's art is one of construction and reconstruction, of collection and recollection. In his beautifully meticulous photographs we are presented with various tableaux, each made from paper and cardboard, which seem at once familiar and yet devoid of identifying details. Cardboard boxes are piled up, yet there is nothing printed upon them that would betray either their contents or indeed any details of their transportation; similarly, an office desk is covered by a deluge of ransacked papers, although they are mutely blank. Although the places themselves may seem blandly generic – an office, a table primed for a press conference, a polling booth – they are taken from recent political events, although recreated without any of the distinguishing marks that might otherwise render them simple copies. Murder, ethnic hatred, corruption: these are the results of decisions taken and speeches made in such anonymous places, tragedies brought about by a thinking, but unfeeling, bureaucracy.

Demand's short film *Hof (Yard)* presents a similarly anonymous tale. We hear footsteps as photographers' flashbulbs illuminate a fenced-off entranceway. The visual style is reminiscent in some respects of *film noir*, and creates a certain amount of suspense, most plainly because we find ourselves within a narrative about which we know nothing: Where are we? Whose footsteps are these? Whose point of view is this? Is someone being closed down here, and if so are we the hunter, or the hunted? The flashing that illuminates the scene is a witty aside on the role of the camera in the construction of history. In Demand's work, political events, part of both place and history, are reconstructed in such a manner that the specifics of both are erased, leaving almost a pattern of political manoeuvres that can be stamped upon any given situation.

Hof (Yard)
Thomas Demand, 2002

Appearances can be deceptive – and often deceptively simple – and this is certainly true of Sharon Lockhart's film *Teatro Amazonas* – a static thirty-minute shot that looks out from the stage of the Amazonas Theatre in Manaus, Brazil, onto the 308 cast members seated in the auditorium. The construction of the piece, however, is far more complex. The cast was made up entirely from residents of the town, chosen with the help of professional anthropologists and official statisticians to represent the demographics of the town and its constituent neighbourhoods. In sympathy with the visual nature of the film, the soundtrack is simple too, a live performance by a chorus of sixty voices of a minimalist composition that consists of the vowels 'a, e, i, o, u' sung in Portuguese. The setting also betrays its colonial roots, the theatre being Manaus's greatest architectural landmark, a symbol of the region's golden age at the close of the nineteenth century and built in a hybrid style of elegant lines and high baroque. With an understated elegance, this film shows a building that represents a time, and a people that represents a place, while simultaneously presenting the difficulties of all forms of representation, whether politically or aesthetically.

'Many communitarians seem to believe that we belong to only one community, defined empirically and even geographically, and that this community could be unified by a single idea of the common good. But we are in fact always multiple and contradictory subjects, inhabitants of a diversity of communities (as many, really, as the social relations in which we participate and the subject-positions they define), constructed by a variety of discourses and precariously and temporarily sutured at the intersection of those positions.'
Chantal Mouffe

Teatro Amazonas
Sharon Lockhart, 1999

Dammi i colori is a single-channel video work by the Albanian artist Anri Sala that explores the transformative effect of politics upon a sense of place. Created as a form of subjective documentary, the video looks at one aspect of the work of the flamboyant mayor of the Albanian capital Tirana, the former artist Edi Rama, who has held the post since October 2000. His most visible effect has been the cleaning up of the city, both in terms of political corruption and also the indiscriminate clearing of illegally constructed buildings and kiosks on municipal land such as parks and river banks (indeed, the latter building work was often the result of the former corruption). This 'Return to Identity' project, and the 'Clean and Green' project of 2000, have resulted in the production of nearly 100,000 square metres of green land in the city, and the planting of 1,800 trees. It is to a different, related project that Sala turns his attention, however: the painting of many crumbling apartment and office blocks in patterns of acidic yellows, greens and purples, which have become known as Edi Rama colours. Through the fifteen minutes of the video, we travel through the city at night in the company of the mayor, as he describes his belief in the construction of a new sense of community and civic purpose that is being generated through the use of vivacious colour, an expression of the utopian belief in the power of art to transform the world for the better. However, one cannot help but sense a certain degree of ambivalence within the work to this admittedly laudable position. The video is not produced in the manner of a corporate promotion, but is rather more 'rough-cut' in style. And by shooting most of the video at night, the strong artificial lighting heightens the unnaturalness of the colours, as if they – and the beliefs that they symbolize – are in some way made strange.

For his campaign for re-election in October 2003, Rama recorded a rap song called 'Tirona', the slang name for the capital city, with one of Albania's leading hip-hop bands, West Side Family:

'This is the city where mosques and churches are built side by side / This is the place where the snobs with Rolex watches go to the gypsy market / This is the place of disillusions where dreams become reality / Here is where you meet a mayor shouting down a megaphone / Where anything can happen / Where not just the women but also the façades of buildings can wear make-up.'
Edi Rama

Hellersdorf Story

In the 1970s when I grew up in the GDR (before my family tried to flee the country), everyone looked with great envy at those who lived in a modern building in (East) Berlin. It was the greatest luxury to have a flat in one of the high-rise buildings – central heating, lifts, and dustbins that run like wells from the top floor down to the cellar. At that time old houses were of an extremely low standard because the state didn't invest in the old, only in the new. The main argument for building whole new districts for thousands of people overnight was a 'big housing shortage' (later proved to have been a false assumption). One of the last and most highly ambitious GDR building projects took place in Hellersdorf.

Hellersdorf is a suburb of former East Berlin. It has officially existed since 1 June 1986. Until then, this area north-east of Berlin was pretty much untouched. Due to its special soil, its masses of boulders deposited by the glaciers of the ice age, and the direction of the prevailing wind, some hundred years ago the fields of Hellersdorf had became a gigantic sewage dump for Berlin. Now a satellite town of 44,000 apartments for at least 100,000 people was to be built there within five years.

All possible resources from the entire Republic – tools, materials, professional builders and building cooperatives of the different cities and regions – were gathered together to build up this new district. Each region was assigned to fulfil a specific part of the building plan. Later on, this became part of the history of Hellersdorf. Those in the know can identify the buildings by colour, the grain and the style of their prefabricated concrete elements as being 'typical Rostock', 'Magdeburg', 'Cottbus'... – also street names and nicknames for houses and places recall the builders' origins.

When just a few houses were finished and the whole surrounding area was still a big construction site, young families already began to move in. Most were happy with their new and modern apartments, but some had had no choice and had been sent there by the state-run housing office. During the first few years the inhabitants had to deal with numerous difficulties: the new underground line from Alexanderplatz was not yet finished; playgrounds, supermarkets, and schools were still missing; the streets and the surrounding landscape were a big muddy mess. However this didn't really matter. It brought the people closer together, made them feel like they were an active and important part in the process of constructing their new society. Early on the 'Hellersdorfers' formed all kinds of collective associations (a widespread habit in the GDR) in order to contribute to their new living area. History and archaeology workshops were founded as well as all kinds of nature conservation organizations and culture clubs. Every little trace and source that could be used to enrich the 'Hellersdorf story' and to support the local identification process was keenly seized up on.

In 1989 when Germany was re-united, construction work at Hellersdorf was still in full progress. By the 1990s it was already deemed necessary to renovate most of the buildings, and the surroundings were adapted to a 'western standard'; international architecture and art competitions were carried out to brighten up the area, to design contemporary urban features. Hellersdorf was given a city centre, 'Helle Mitte' (Bright Centre), including a town hall, a variety of shopping arcades, a multiplex cinema and schools. It tries hard to be another Potsdamer Platz, only smaller.

I became interested in Hellersdorf through an invitation to a public art competition. It was for a high school for medical professions located in the new centre. I wanted to refer to the past (the 'pre-history') of the developed area. I suggested creating a garden of drawings representing wildly growing local plants. The school yard was to have big drawings inlaid into the concrete so as to form an uncontrolled wilderness. As a further connection to the natural history, I intended to install a group of huge boulders to sit on, lean against, hang out around. In contrast to the chaotic outside, the stone floor of the school lobby was to show the plant drawings systematically organized like a sort of encyclopaedic garden, with generic names attached. I won the competition, but for different reasons the project was never carried out.

For this book I have made a photo series in two parts. One part comes from the Hellersdorf ten-year jubilee magazine and shows sites during the building process – part of the self-mythologizing process. Recently I returned to Hellersdorf to see what these places look like today, and to photograph them again.

Katrin von Maltzahn, June 2002

Trotz dieser »historischen Behinderungen« konnte die
erste Platte am 26. September 1984 im Magdeburger

traurige Wahrzeichen des abgebrochenen Großprojektes.

Willie Doherty was born in 1959 in Derry, Northern Ireland, a place of conflicting histories, religious and political (apparent even to the extent that it has two competing names, as it also known as Londonderry). In some early works, black-and-white photographs of the city were presented with words printed upon their surface, in a manner reminiscent of artists such as Richard Long or Hamish Fulton. Rather than the personal transformations experienced by these often solitary walkers, however, Doherty's images emphasized this urban landscape as one saturated with political meaning and conflict, where to walk from one place to another could be seen as an act of aggression or provocation, and as a consequence as either noble or foolhardy.

Doherty's more recent work *Extracts from a File* was made in Berlin, a city that was itself famously divided by opposing ideologies. Now able to roam unrestricted, the artist moves through the city at night, in Doherty's hands, a city without recognizable landmarks that consists, instead, of fragments captured from the surrounding darkness, a world glimpsed quickly through a viewfinder like an act of covert surveillance, although the film's purpose remains as uncertain as the activities that may – or may not – be taking place within these illuminated interiors. It is a work that exudes a cold, sweaty paranoia, which depends upon our knowledge of Berlin and our inability to place these pictures with any exactitude. We read them in relation, then, to the Berlin of our imagination and memory, a city of films and photographs, and therefore a place that may never have actually existed.

this page and opposite
Extracts from a File
Willie Doherty, 2000

In Germany, there are more than 260 roads, streets and paths whose names refer to a Jewish presence, and for *The J-Street Project*, Susan Hiller visited them all. Making numerous journeys, Hiller filmed and took photographs of these evocative places, whether inner-city shopping streets, anonymous suburbs or secluded country roads, in an attempt to trace the absence that is explicitly named on maps and street signs. These places might seem ordinary – as might the images themselves – but through these names, both are invested with an historical richness that speaks eloquently of the past, and how that past makes its mark upon our contemporary lives.

**Judengasse,
Pretzfeld**
Susan Hiller, 2002–3

'The sign is usually said to be put in the place of the thing itself, the present thing, "thing" here standing equally for meaning or referent. The sign represents the present in its absence. It takes the place of the present. When we cannot grasp or show the thing, state the present, the being "present" when the present cannot be presented, we signify, we go through the detour of the sign. We give or take signs. We signal. The sign, in this sense, is deferred presence.'
Jacques Derrida

top left
Judengasse, Altenburg
Susan Hiller, 2002–3

top right
**Jüdenstrasse,
Weissenfels**
Susan Hiller, 2002–3

bottom left
Judengraben, Kronach
Susan Hiller, 2002–3

bottom right
Judenhain, Marienburg
Susan Hiller, 2002–3

'The formal elements of any Greek sanctuary are, first, the specifically sacred landscape in which it is set and, second, the buildings that are placed within it. The landscape and the temples together form the architectural whole.... Each [such] sanctuary differs from all others because it is in a different place.'

Vincent Scully

It might be said that architecture is society's values made concrete, and as such it has proven an important foundation upon which Nathan Coley has built his practice. Often highly discursive in form, Coley's works initiate a simple line of enquiry in order to test how society structures its beliefs, and whether the forms that surround us might become redundant – or reassigned – should those beliefs change. When commissioned to produce a public art work by a gallery in Edinburgh, for example, Coley proposed the construction of an urban sanctuary. In order to develop the project, Coley interviewed a number of professionals – a theologian, an architect, a chief superintendent and an artist, among others – to determine not only the form that it might take, but also what it might mean – would the police be able to enter it to arrest a criminal claiming sanctuary, for example? Unknown to those interviewed, the sanctuary was never to be built, the public art work, instead, consisting of a book that contained the discussions, thereby allowing the contemporary urban sanctuary to remain a place of hope and imagination. Of course, sanctuary could be found historically within the confines of a church, a type of building about which Coley has made a number of works, whether constructing cardboard models of all the places of worship within a particular city, or in *Fourteen Churches of Münster*. Our view is from a helicopter passing above the German city; in a beautifully choreographed aerial sweep, our gaze settles upon a church below and we circle it slowly, before moving quickly onto the next. Our attention is not being drawn to them solely for their architectural worth, however; according to the pilot of an Allied bomber during the Second World War, 'The field order was coming in on the teletype and we learned that our target was to be the front steps of Münster Cathedral.' Where once it could save others, the symbolic power of these buildings threatened their own safety.

Fourteen Churches of Münster
Nathan Coley, 2000

'It is not the church we want, but the sacrifice; not the emotion of admiration, but the act of adoration: not the gift, but the giving.'

John Ruskin

The artist Jun Nguyen-Hatsushiba is himself the product of many places – born in Tokyo, educated in America, and now resident in Ho Chi Minh City, Vietnam – and his work also draws upon the relationship between different cultural reference points. In *Memorial Project Nha Trang, Vietnam: Towards the Complex – For the Courageous, the Curious, and the Cowards*, the references are to his adoptive homeland, specifically to two traditional modes of work – fisherman and cyclo (bicycle-taxi) driver. In this languidly beautiful video work, cyclos slowly race each other along the sea bed at Nha Trang, fishermen acting as drivers, holding their breath long enough to propel their vehicle just a few feet further before being forced to the surface while another takes their place. In a country undergoing rapid social and economic development, both the drivers and fishermen find themselves increasingly disenfranchised, and in this poetic work we find them struggling to make progress in an environment that frustrates their actions.

'Just as none of us is outside or beyond geography, none of us is completely free from the struggle over geography.'

Edward Said

Memorial Project Nha Trang, Vietnam: Towards the Complex – For the Courageous, the Curious, and the Cowards
Jun Nguyen-Hatsushiba, 2001

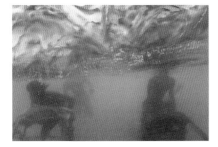

Any place is in fact a layering of other places – that is, the place at different points in its history – and it is this exploration of place that we find in British artist Steve McQueen's two related films, *Caribs' Leap* and *Western Deep*. The first work is shown over two screens; the first, smaller, shows the slow, small details of everyday life on the Caribbean island of Grenada, such as a boat rowing across a stretch of water or coconut shells floating by, their passage less determined, while people stand around and drift through the day. On the larger screen clouds drift too, although our reveries are broken by the image of a man falling through the sky, unnoticed by those going about their everyday activities, much like Icarus's plunge in Breughel's painting *The Fall of Icarus* (1558), so memorably described in W. H. Auden's poem, '*Musée des Beaux Arts*' (1938). It is to an event that took place just over a century after Breughel completed his work that McQueen makes the most explicit reference, however, when in 1651 the native Caribs preferred to jump to their deaths from the cliffs – at a place now called Caribs' Leap – rather than submit to the French, who had bought the island cheaply before driving the natives from their own land. As McQueen has remarked, Grenada has been repopulated five times within three hundred years, his own parents among the inhabitants. Indeed, it was during a recent visit to the island for his grandmother's funeral that he conceived of the film. Following her death, he felt that there was no longer anyone there to hold the place together, and his relationship to it was profoundly altered. It is an elegiac work about the ways in which a sense of tragedy, both personal and historic, descends upon place.

There is a descent, also, in *Western Deep*, perhaps the most documentary-like of all McQueen's works. Filmed inside a South African goldmine, the darkness of the screen is relieved only briefly by the dim flashes of red light as the cage descends the shaft, revealing for a moment the edge of a helmet or part of a face. Deep below the earth, a channel of black oily water spills by and the straining of our vision encourages us to draw out images of other places from the broken rock that emerges from just below the darkness. What is clearly visible, however, is the wretched existence of the miners themselves, especially within their underground 'restroom'. Here the men, exhausted, engage in regimented exercises, stepping up and down upon the metal benches that line the room, while red lights and an insistent buzzer seem to drive their weary limbs. The mine is still operated by the company that did so under apartheid, an exhibition guide informs us, and for all the changes that are visible in the new South Africa, they do not seem to have penetrated below its surface.

top left
**Still from *Caribs' Leap* from
*Caribs' Leap/Western Deep***
Steve McQueen, 2002

left
**Still from *Western Deep* from
*Caribs' Leap/Western Deep***
Steve McQueen, 2002

A Foreign Country by David Vaughan

I knew nothing of Lidice before I moved to Czechoslovakia thirteen years ago. It was only on visits to the neighbouring industrial town of Kladno that I gradually learned of the fate of the village. In the bus I would pass the rusting corrugated iron fence and the half-built twisted metal ruins of the vast memorial and conference centre that the communists had begun to build in the 1980s. With the fall of the regime, work on the hugely out-of-scale project stopped.

Lidice was razed to the ground by the Nazis on 10 June 1942 in retaliation for the assassination of the Nazi deputy ruler of occupied Bohemia and Moravia, Reinhard Heydrich. The men of the village – 173 human souls – were shot against the wall of the Horák family farmhouse. The women and the children were sent to concentration camps. Later 82 of the children were murdered. The women who survived returned to find a field of rye where the village had stood, with a path beaten to the mass grave, where crops grew greener and faster.

A few years ago in a Prague second-hand bookshop, I found a book that the Czechoslovak Interior Ministry had produced in 1945, just months after the end of the war, a document outlining details of the Lidice massacre. I lent the book to an 80-year-old Canadian professor, David Kirk, who was interested in the fate of the Lidice children and had contacted me during a visit to Prague. He pointed out a passing reference that I hadn't noticed

to a film that had been made in Britain during the war by Humphrey Jennings, an attempt to re-create the Lidice tragedy in the context of a Welsh village.

The idea captured my imagination. I arranged to see *The Silent Village* in London and was amazed by what I saw. It was not a historical curiosity, but an extraordinary work of art, a drama without actors, a passion play in which a village takes onto its own shoulders the fate of another village a thousand miles away, not by pretending to be Czech, but by taking the story onto itself. Jennings's film was an over-ambitious and strangely contorted project, that worked through his extraordinary poetic language. 'I would like to be filming trees,' he told Viktor Fischl, the Czech poet who had given him the idea for the film. 'Instead, here I am making a propaganda film.'

The Nazis made their own film of the destruction of Lidice. They used the best Czech documentary cameraman of his generation, Čeněk Zahradniček, threatening him with execution. They re-routed the stream and levelled the uneven parts of the ground. Their efficiency is carefully recorded. These images of Lidice burning have become familiar to every Czech.

In 1999 I put together a programme about *The Silent Village* for Czech Radio, visiting Jennings' chosen village of Cwmgiedd at the head of the Swansea Valley. I travelled through Wales with the countryside around Kladno in my mind. I couldn't help looking

Film still from
The Silent Village, *1943*
Courtesy of the British Film Institute

for similarities, and, of course, I found as many or as few as the mood of the moment.

In the Art Nouveau café of the Obecni dum in Prague, I met Viktor Fischl. He is 90, lives in Jerusalem, and today is one of the grand old men of Czech letters.

'The voice of the seedlings under the furrow,
of the young shoots driving up into the spring,
of the green buds born from the trunk's mutilations.'

He told me of the long poem *The Dead Village* which he had written hours after he heard of the Lidice massacre from his wartime exile in London. The poem gave him the idea for *The Silent Village*, as a way for the people of Britain to *identify* with the fate of occupied Europe. This was what Humphrey Jennings then tried to achieve. Viktor Fischl believes he succeeded, that the villagers of Cwmgiedd *'lived Lidice'.* Today we cannot know. All we have is the film.

In Cwmgiedd, *The Silent Village* has become part of the identity of the village. A whole generation of villagers appeared in the film. A moment in the village's history is captured. People see themselves when young, or their parents and grandparents, growing a little more distant each time they see the film.

I watched the film with Mair Thomas in the living room behind her family's butcher's shop in Cwmgiedd. *'It sends a shiver down*

my spine to see them. All dead.' She is talking of the villagers of Cwmgiedd, her relatives from 60 years ago. Perhaps she is also talking of the people whose fate they are enacting. If I were to ask she would probably not be sure. Most of the actors of Cwmgiedd have now joined the men and children of Lidice. She recites passages from the film from memory.

'I have just had a letter to inform me that there is no more Welsh to be spoken in this school…. But, children, I want you to promise me one thing. Do not forget your Welsh. Speak Welsh at home, on the roadside, at your play, everywhere. Will you promise me not to forget your Welsh language?'
'Yes, Miss Daniels.'

Ewart Alexander was a little boy at the Cynlais School. We see him being taken away with the other children to a waiting Gestapo truck. He grew up to be a writer and has written two plays about *The Silent Village*. In the second, which he wrote shortly after my first visit to Cwmgiedd three years ago, a villager from Cwmgiedd meets a survivor from Lidice, in a meeting characterized by tension and then reconciliation. I have visited Ewart several times. With nostalgia he recalls memories from the filming, but each time he repeats the memories they satisfy him less. The thought of the *other people*, the victims of the real atrocity in that other place

Wynne Horák, Pavla Nešporová and Anna Nešporová by the ruins of the Horák farmhouse
From *The Second Life of Lidice*, 2001

will not go away. It adds unease to nostalgia for a summer of filming 60 years ago.

A booklet was produced in 1943 to accompany the premiere of *The Silent Village*. In his introduction, the then Czechoslovak foreign minister in exile, Jan Masaryk, wrote that two men of Lidice were not murdered. They were airmen in the RAF and one of them had married a Welsh girl.

In fact she was English. Perhaps her name – Wynne – sounded Welsh to Masaryk, perhaps it was just licence. Her husband was Josef Horák from Lidice, a pilot in the Czechoslovak 311 Squadron.

When Pavel Štingl and I were working on our film *The Second Life of Lidice,* we had little difficulty finding Wynne. Before I even knew of *The Silent Village* I had interviewed her sister-in-law, Anna Nešporová, in Lidice. Anna Nešporová was one of the women of Lidice who had survived. Apart from her

brother in England, all her family had been shot, and it was against the barn of her family's farm that the 173 men of the village were murdered. In May 1945 Anna walked 300 kilometres home from Ravensbrück. She is small and extraordinarily strong. Anna always stands as she talks of the events of the war – sometimes up to four hours as she remembers details.

Wynne is tall and dignified. She is what Czechs would call a '*dáma*'. The English word 'lady' would be a woefully inadequate translation. Wynne has never lost the beauty of her youth, and it is easy to imagine her with her handsome young Czech pilot husband. She lives in Stratton-St-Margaret, on the outskirts of Swindon.

In the weeks after the war, Josef, Wynne and their two sons moved straight to Czechoslovakia. The boys had never seen Lidice and at first played in the field of rye. They were the only intact Lidice family. Lidice women were slowly trickling back from Ravensbrück, and gradually 17 surviving children were found.

Within three years Wynne and her family – the last people of Lidice to bear the name Horák – were driven out of Czechoslovakia. It was a grotesque twist of fate, shared by many

TERRITORIES

The politics of place are made manifest through different groups' territorial claims. Often people fight to maintain these divides or to dissolve them completely. Others try simply to slip through them undetected. These are the marks of ideology upon the earth. Some artists reflect and reflect upon these territorial battles; others explore the absurdities that can occur in the demarcation of such spaces. But what of those who choose to live on the land nomadically, without making a claim on it?

For many years now the Scottish artist Ross Sinclair has been engaged in an extraordinarily wide-ranging and ambitious project that might be loosely defined, borrowing the title from one of his recent publications, as 'Real Life and How to Live It'. Perhaps the greatest impediments to living a 'Real Life', in Sinclair's terms, are various forms of state apparatus and the knowledge structures that act as their foundations, whether it be 'Parliament' or 'History'; Sinclair resists any simplistic call for their dismantling or abolition, however, but rather initiates a process of re-imagining what these structures – architectural and philosophical – might become ('Not as it is but as it could be', as the wall text in one of his installations declares).

This re-imagining took place on a massive scale in his installation *Journey to the Edge of the World – The New Republic of St Kilda* at The Fruitmarket Gallery in Edinburgh, approximately one hundred yards from the newly established Scottish Parliament. The islands of St Kilda, by contrast, lie one hundred miles west of the British mainland, seventeen hours by boat from Oban, and were, until their evacuation in 1930, the most remote inhabited part of the United Kingdom. Every morning a meeting would take place in order to make all the important decisions of the day, although this was no simple matter of voting, as each issue was discussed – sometimes at length – until a consensus was reached. Life was organized differently in many other important ways: there was no money and no crime (and so no police) and no calendar and no clocks. As contact with the mainland increased during the nineteenth century, however, the St Kildans' way of life became increasingly threatened, by organized education and religion, and then by disease. Less than one hundred years of contact with the modern world destroyed a society that had survived over one thousand years of isolation.

Sinclair uses this sorry tale as the starting point to imagine what the New Republic of St Kilda might be, how it might be brought about, and what we might learn from its constitution. Around the space we can hear Sinclair singing traditional Scottish songs and hymns, although here the recordings are played backwards, as if to emphasize the malevolent influence of mainstream culture upon St Kilda's development, and the misplaced sense of progress that destroys what it cannot easily assimilate. Sinclair's structures possess a strong sense of 'making do', of being temporary, of existing as long as is necessary but never so long that they might then dictate what is possible, or impossible. The new parliament, then, becomes an area of stacked cardboard boxes, stepped, upon which people might sit and discuss the matter at hand. Elsewhere, a large blackboard hangs upon a wall, the word 'GEOGRAPHY' painted across its width; behind the text in white chalk is drawn a map of the world although it has been rotated one-hundred-and-eighty-degrees so that it is, according to cartographic convention, 'upside down'. Sinclair has made it even more difficult to read, however: it is the Pacific Ocean, rather than the Atlantic, which is found towards the map's centre and the few words of text that denote chosen countries have been laterally-reversed, as if seen in a mirror, or as if we are standing in the imaginary space behind the map itself. All is either upside-down or the wrong way round, and the only state of which we can be certain is a state of confused dislocation. An arrow points to ADLIK TS, now hidden behind a box. Indeed, cardboard boxes line the gallery walls completely, hiding their supposed institutional neutrality. Sinclair has succeeded in creating a space of simple constructions that construct something far more complex, a space that appears in some sense transient, and also a space of repository, where the St Kildans' culture and spirit is kept safe, awaiting its chance to be used once more.

Journey to the Edge of the World – The New Republic of St Kilda
Ross Sinclair, 1999

Perhaps some of the lessons learned from *Journey to the Edge of the World* can be found in subsequent works, such as *Real Life and How to Live it, No. 1 – Geography*, which was installed on the side of a building in Leipzig. During his visits to Leipzig, which was part of the former East Germany, Sinclair had often seen murals painted upon the ends of buildings that extolled the virtues of the Communist system. Rather old-fashioned, and beautiful perhaps because of this, these murals were quickly disappearing in the massive reconstruction of the city, to be replaced by the saturation imagery of capitalist advertising. Sinclair created a new mural that drew on both traditions in order to create a new mental space in which the viewer might then be allowed to consider a new political space, a space no doubt different from the geographic and political changes already underway in this place. We'd be foolish to accept Sinclair's list as a simple strategy to adopt in order to achieve 'Real Life', however, as it is left completely undecided as to whether Sinclair is suggesting that we do, or do not, follow the guide and the actions that it contains. It seems that 'Real Life' can only ever be achieved through a process of active negotiation rather than passive acceptance.

'The modern "murals" of capitalism are computer-generated and are printed on fine mesh which is then stretched over the building in use. However, I wanted my mural to hark back to the pedagogic, dogmatic certainty of the previous era, painted directly onto the surface of the wall. Although the population are far from nostalgic for Soviet times, there is a strange feeling that while things were bad, at least there was full employment and the DDR world was a far safer and simpler place. The entreaties of the communist era are rapidly being replaced by the mantra of late capitalism, with the usual Gap, McDonalds and Nike stores elegantly displaying their manifesto. I wanted to propose a new idea, but in this old medium about which the people were strangely sentimental.'
Ross Sinclair

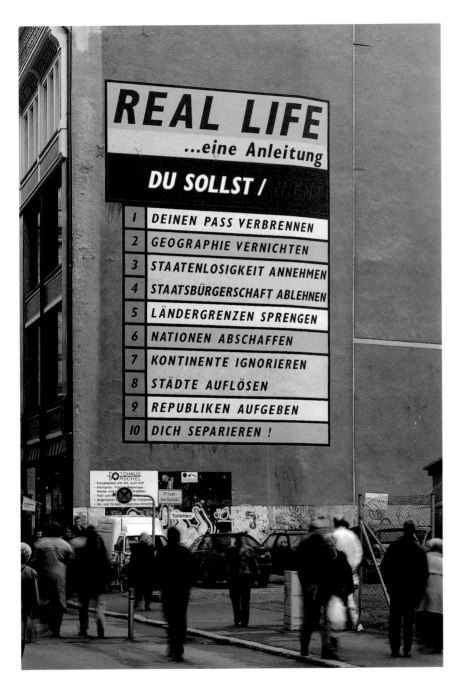

Real Life and How to Live
it, No. 1 – Geography
Ross Sinclair, 2000

For over thirty years, the Belgian director Chantal Akerman has been making films that reveal a fascination with the rhythms of everyday life. In *Jeanne Dielman, 23 quai du Commerce, 1080 Bruxelles* (1975), the film that brought the young Akerman critical acclaim at the Cannes Film Festival, we are presented with a portrait of both the person (played by Delphine Seyrig) and place of the title, and the daily routines that the one undertakes in the other. There is a persistence of vision in this film that has become typical of Akerman's work, a respectful distance that allows events to unfold in their own time whether it is, in the case of *Jeanne Dielman…*, the peeling of potatoes or a fatal stabbing. In *D'Est* (From the East) (1993) the inhabitants of Russia and Eastern Europe are afforded the same respect as the heroine in Akerman's early masterpiece. As she wrote in advance of shooting the film:

'While there's still time, I would like to make a grand journey across Eastern Europe. To Russia, Poland, Hungary, Czechoslovakia, the former East Germany, and back to Belgium.

I'd like to film there, in my own style of documentary bordering on fiction. I'd like to shoot everything. Everything that moves me.

Faces, streets, cars going by and buses, train stations and plains, rivers and oceans, streams and brooks, trees and forests. Fields and factories and yet more faces. Food, interiors, doors, windows, meals being prepared. Women and men, young and old, people passing by or at rest, seated or standing, even lying down. Days and nights, wind and rain, snow and springtime.

And everything I see along the way that is slowly changing – faces and landscapes. All these countries in the throes of great change. Countries that have shared a common history since the war and are still deeply marked by this history, even in the very contours of the earth. Countries now embarking on different paths.'

In 1995, the feature-length *D'Est* was transformed into a gallery-based installation, Akerman's first, and this is a form of presentation that she has subsequently explored with *From the Other Side*. The other side in question here, one presumes, is Agua Prieta, Sonora, a small town over the American–Mexican border from Douglas, Arizona, where Mexicans come and wait before making the hazardous journey into the mountains and deserts of Arizona. Here, place is transformed into territory, as the Immigration and Naturalization Services maintain an extraordinary vigilance over the terrain, employing visual technologies perfected during the first Gulf War to detect the passage of attempted immigrants, thereby pushing them further into more hostile environments. As some inhabitants of Douglas betray their own fears and prejudices in interviews – the infections of crime and disease the most common fears they have of outsiders – a local sheriff remarks that the government's crackdown is a 'bad strategy and a bad plan', calling the elevated death toll that results from the now more dangerous crossing 'a calculated consequence'. A live real-time broadcast from the region itself shows the desolate landscape, divided by a running fence, and subject to surveillance.

From the Other Side
Chantal Akerman, 2002

Irish artist Kathy Prendergast s work – whether sculpture or drawing – has for many years explored the potential for commonplace domestic objects to possess an emotional weight far beyond their mere physical one. The transformations are often unsettling, redolent of those undertaken by the Surrealists, such as long tresses of hair sweeping from an old worn table, an accompanying chair having strands of hair sewn into its cushion too. Prendergast's interest in 'making strange' the world around us undertook a dramatic shift in scale in 1992 when she began an ambitious new series of works, *City Drawings* (1992–ongoing), in which she set out to make delicate pencil drawings of all the world's major capital cities (there will be one hundred and eighty drawings in the series, when complete). The size of the paper on which each drawing is made remains constant – 24 x 32 cm – and the cities occupy the same area within this sheet regardless of their actual size, from the sprawling megalopolises of Seoul or London to the rather more accessible Yaren in Nauru, or Funafuti in Tuvalu. While maps are always a form of abstraction, Prendergast has exaggerated this characteristic by removing all place names and signs of parks, buildings or other facilities that might give meaning, or a sense of utility. Instead the lines of the streets cross and wind around one another, swerving, curving, revealing, in their delicate beauty, the underlying patterns of the cities themselves, the huddled medieval town centre or the gridded new world, like topographic versions of the earliest memories laid down in the brain, whose dendrites and fibres these drawings so clearly resemble.

In some sense, then, these drawings seem to suggest the process by which the city is absorbed by the person making their way through it; in memorizing it, the city is mapped in miniature in the connected cells of the brain. In a more recent series, *Between Love and Paradise* (2002), and also in *Lost* (1999), we perhaps see the complementary action. Here Prendergast has taken a digital map of North America and, while keeping basic topographic information such as state borders and major roadways, has removed all place names, with the exception of those that have some connection with emotions or other similar characteristics, such as 'Surprise', 'Defiance', or 'Love Hollow'. *Lost* retains only those place names that begin with the word 'lost', such as 'Lost Creek', 'Lost Island' and 'Lost Canyon'. The viewer is uncertain what is being described here: are these names of actual places, or descriptions of things that have now disappeared? Is it less a picture of a nation state than of a state of mind? With a great economy of means, Prendergast exposes the paradox that lies at the heart of the mapmaking process, and by extension any attempted understanding of the world around us: that what is found is seldom equivalent to what has been lost.

'For the last few years I have been researching place names with the idea of producing an "Emotional Atlas of the World". This atlas would show all the places in the world which have names connected with emotions, i.e. Lost Bay, Lonely Island, Hearts Desire, etc., rather than the conventional atlas which shows places of importance. The map *Lost*…is a variation on this theme, showing all the "lost" places in North America. Until quite recently maps and atlases were produced by hand. Within the last few years new atlases have been produced using digital technology. It is the combination of this technology, the place-name information on the internet and my idea that has made this project possible.'
Kathy Prendergast

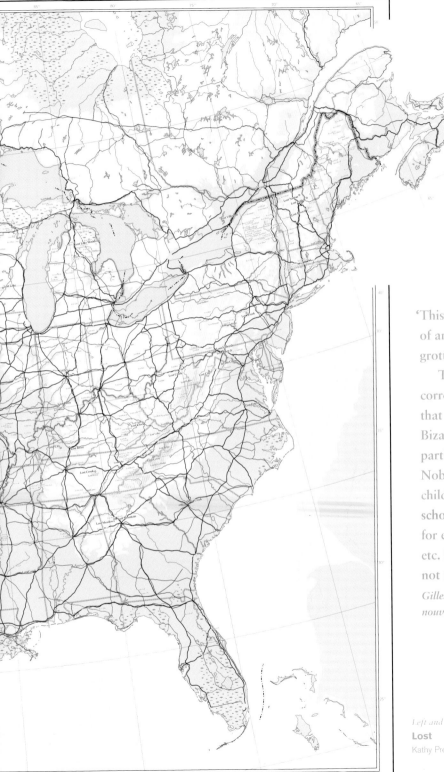

'This town could be envisaged in the form of an arbitrary grouping of chateaux, grottoes, lakes, etc.

The quarters of this city could correspond to diverse catalogued feelings that one meets by chance in current life. Bizarre Quarter – Happy Quarter – particularly reserved for habitation – Noble and Tragic Quarter (for wise children) – Historic Quarter (museums, schools) – Useful Quarter (shops, shops for equipment) – Sinister Quarter etc., etc. Perhaps also a Quarter of Death, not to die in but to live in peace.'

Gilles Ivain, 'Formulaire pour un urbanisme nouveau', Internationale situationniste 1 (June 1958)

Left and previous page

Lost
Kathy Prendergast, 1999

The Kingdoms of Elgaland–Vargaland

With effect from the 14th March 1992, we are annexing and occupying the following territories:

I. All border frontier areas between all countries on earth, and all areas (up to a width of 10 nautical miles) existing outside all countries' territorial waters. We designate these territories our physical territory.

II. Mental and perceptive territories such as the Hypnagogue State (civil), the Escapistic Territory (civil) and the Virtual Room (digital).

On the 27th of May 1992 at 12 noon GMT, we proclaimed the state of Elgaland-Vargaland.

Leif Elggren
founder of Elgaland

CM von Hausswolff
founder of Vargaland

It is said that Sweden was one of only eight countries in the world that did not have its government or borders changed by undemocratic means in the twentieth century (even in the last decade or so of that century, war and political upheaval brought about the creation, or re-creation, of numerous states). It was within the relative political stability of Stockholm, then, that in 1992 the formation of another country was formally announced.

The proclamation was made four times (once each in the North, South, East and West) by the founders and rulers of The Kingdoms of Elgaland-Vargaland, the Swedish artists Leif Elggren and Carl Michael von

Hausswolff, or Leif I and Michael I, as they are more regally addressed.

Later that year, a constitution was published containing details of the state's government, citizen's rights ('f: everything and more; g: nothing and less'), its flag, coats of arms, anthem, as well as the national dish (pasta in sunflower oil, tomato ketchup and crushed garlic with basil) and drink (vodka and Coca-Cola). More recently, at the 2003 Venice Biennale, the Kingdoms of Elgaland-Vargaland annexed Utopia into their territories, and published an edition of Thomas More's establishing work by way of commemoration.

An exploration of 'vulnerability, hierarchies, nationalism, manipulation, madness, and normality', Elgaland-Vargaland is ruled by those who have adopted a position of absolute power in order that they can then absolve themselves of it, a manic control that must then begin to slip. The state *as* art compels us to explore the state *of* art.

'The project Mongolia consists of images of landscapes, portraits of the nomads outdoors and inside their *gers* and portraits of the *gers* in the landscape. A *ger* is a round, white tent and is the home of the nomads living on the steppes in Mongolia. For almost 3,000 years the shape and the function of the *ger* has remained the same. It is also known as a *jurte*, originally a Turkish name and also used in the Russian and the German language. For this project I travelled for six weeks in a rented jeep through Mongolia, from the Gobi Desert in the south to the Khenti region in the north, the area where Genghis Khan was born 800 years ago.'
Mette Tronvoll

top left
Ger 001
Mette Tronvoll, 2003

top right
Ger 002
Mette Tronvoll, 2003

bottom left
Ger 003
Mette Tronvoll, 2003

bottom right
The Purews, Luwsansharaws and Dulamsuren Otschir
Mette Tronvoll, 2003

'The nomad moves, but he is always at the centre of the desert, at the centre of the steppe.'

Gaston Bachelard

'For dwelling-as-residing is not necessarily sedentary; not the literal absence of motion but finding a relatively stable place in the world is what matters in such dwelling. Such finding is possible even when in motion. The earth offers continual if sometimes uncomfortable accommodations as one moves across its surface. If human beings may peregrinate in place, so they may also dwell stably even as they move from place to place.'

Edward S. Casey

ITINERANCY

Is it possible to find a dwelling, a place within the world, while moving across it?
We are fixated with property claims and the possibility of embedding ourselves
and of finding our identity in our surroundings. But if identity itself is fluid, the identity
of place as much as that of ourselves, is it not natural to be in a constant state of
movement rather than standing still? In a world of global exchange,
perhaps we are all of us always moving.

Like much of the work of Belgian artist Francis Alÿs *When Faith Moves Mountains* is a work of great simplicity and poetic richness. Alÿs first visited Lima for the Biennial in 2000 and was struck by the desperate situation he found there; the Fujimori government was on the brink of collapse – it was to do so the following year – and the city was in turmoil with street clashes and general unrest. Such unrest was not new however: it had followed the civil war fought during the 1980s and 1990s between the military and various guerrilla groups. The fighting had displaced a great many people, who now made their homes in shanty towns situated on the enormous sand dunes that surround the city, a situation that suggested the competing actions of dispersal and cohesion in both the natural and social realms, and which, in Alÿs's words, 'called for an "epic response", a "beau geste" at once futile and heroic, absurd and urgent'.

The place in which Alÿs decided to make this gesture was on the Ventanilla dunes, where more than seventy thousand people live with no electricity or running water. On 11 April 2002, five hundred volunteers were given a shovel and formed a single line at the foot of a giant dune; the group pushed the sand and this sixteen-hundred-foot-long sand dune moved about four inches from its original position. Although in many ways a poetic gesture – one might imagine such an event in a short story by Borges – it was not a literary fiction but, as Alÿs insists, really happened – the dune moved. It may have only been by a small amount – although it may have taken years for such a movement to occur naturally – but it was far enough for it to have entered into local history and the mythology of the place.

American land artist Robert Smithson said that one pebble moving one foot in two million years was enough action to keep him really excited, and one can only imagine what he would have made of this work. For Alÿs, Smithson's land art – for example, his celebrated *Spiral Jetty* in Utah – was closely aligned to civil engineering, whereas his own practice is a civil engineering of a different sort – perhaps an engineering of the civil. As he has remarked, 'Here, we have attempted to create a kind of Land art for the land-less'.

'*When Faith Moves Mountains* attempts to translate social tensions into narratives that in turn intervene in the imaginal landscape of a place.'
Francis Alÿs

**Cuando la fe mueve montañas, Lima, Perú,
April 11, 2002
(When Faith Moves Mountains, Lima, Peru,
April 11, 2002)**
Francis Alÿs, 2002

Curator and critic Kitty Scott has described Canadian artist Janet Cardiff as someone 'whose work has no name: she is not a painter, sculptor, or an installation artist'. Indeed, Cardiff hovers in an indefinable place somewhere between film, theatre, radio, literature and performance art, borrowing from each discipline, but never fully inhabiting any one of them. Since the early 1990s, she has become well known for producing haunting yet compelling 'audio-walks'. For these productions, which last from ten to forty minutes, she begins by writing a script that reads like a cross between murder mystery, thriller detective novel, *film noir* and popular science fiction. She then dramatizes the fiction by 'acting it out' on location, inflecting it with the character of a specific place, and all the time recording the spoken narrative on tape as she moves through the chosen locale. For *The Missing Voice (case study b)*, the story was set and performed in London's East End, beginning in the Whitechapel Library and eventually ending up at Liverpool Street station.

Once finished, Cardiff's audio-walks are then re-presented within a gallery space, the spectator, or 'walker', needing headphones, a tape or disc player, and an environment in which to re-create the walk. Cardiff herself plays a central role in these psychologically absorbing fictions, her distinct, softly spoken Canadian voice being her own seductive signature style. At the beginning of each walk, she speaks directly to you: 'Go down the stairs', she might say, or 'Let's walk again'. As a result, the experience is like sharing someone else's meditations or dreamlike thoughts. You feel the effects of loss, misrecognition, incomprehensibility, and the impossibility of communication. At the same time, the more involved you become, the more you realize that the power of these walks resides in your own perceptions. You are central to the story, because it happens in your head. You unwittingly become a performer who completes the circuit, both literally and metaphorically. Cardiff implicates you emotionally and environmentally. Her voice leads. You follow.

you can hear the turning of newspaper pages
people talking softly
there's a man standing beside me
he's looking at the crime section now
he reaches to pick up a book opens it
leafs through a few pages and puts it back on the shelf
[...]
I want you to walk with me there are some things I need to show you
go to the right walk past the main desk through the turnstile
I'm going to go outside
try to follow the sound of my footsteps so that we can stay together
I'm going to turn right onto Whitechapel High Street
turn to the right
past the Whitechapel Art Gallery
[...]
let's go on
she walks up Brick Lane she wears a dark coat and a beige scarf
she looks in the windows as she passes the stores
she knows that his office is close by
turn left onto Brick Lane follow the sidewalk up
I'm behind someone else now
a new companion
they have a duffel coat running shoes red shopping bag
I like not talking to anybody all day
except when I pay for a book or a cup of tea or something
it's like you're invisible
[...]
keep walking straight
cross over to Liverpool Street Station watch out for cars here
go to the entrance beside McDonalds
up the stairs past these weird lights
there's a man in a black suit walking behind you
go over to the metal railing to the right of the white pole
there's a woman with a suitcase standing beneath us looking up the
notice board
[...]
she's getting on the train
he runs along the platform just as it's pulling out of the station
she sees his face in the window and tries to hide
as the train picks up speed she turns her head to watch him fade
into the distance
I have to leave now
I wanted to walk you back to the library but there's not enough time
please return the discman as soon as possible
goodbye

**The Missing Voice
(case study b)**
Janet Cardiff, 1999

Untitled (Demonstration No. 3)
Rirkrit Tiravanija, 2001

Rirkrit Tiravanija's artistic practice has long been one founded upon the making of small gestures, albeit gestures that open, unfolding, amongst people and over time, and attain an increased significance in doing so. It is not simply the spirit that is generous within his work, but usually the actions themselves: Tiravanija has often cooked large meals for all-comers, for example, a personal activity which becomes a collective activity, and which, through his use of specific ingredients – noodles in Venice, for example – extends from the immediate experience of time and place to one of greater cultural, geographic and historical distance. For the Yokohama Triennial in 2001, Tiravanija and a young Japanese artist drove a van from a gallery – the CCA Kitakyushu – to Yokohama, making their way alongside major rivers and bodies of water. Their van was equipped for extreme fishing and camping, and this is what they did for the duration of the twenty-one days of their meandering journey, stopping to meet notable local fishermen, and to fish themselves while enjoying the spectacular countryside. The entire journey was captured by a continuously running video camera mounted in the van, and the resulting video was then put on display in the exhibition. These images were later sequenced into frames and published in the book *Passage Cosmo to Fishy Travels*. The van is still in Japan, fully operational, waiting for fishing trips to come.

'When I was nineteen years old I left Thailand and went to Canada. At that point, I left high school thinking I would go into photojournalism because I enjoyed the idea of being mobile and travelling a lot. I wanted to see everything, and this was a situation that could put me there. I wasn't ever interested in making a lot of money; I just wanted to get by. But I wanted to see everything.'
Rirkrit Tiravanija

'The train from London to Birmingham takes two hours, but I made the trip by boat on a canal built in the eighteenth century, taking two weeks. During this trip, I made pickled vegetables. The vegetables and cucumbers that I bought fresh in London were pickled by the time I reached Birmingham.

When I conceived of this project I didn't know how to make pickles, but by the end of my trip I had learned something about it and my pickled tomatoes were quite good.

While traveling from London to Birmingham, I got recipes for pickles from other people, and I watched the sheep and water birds and leaves floating in the water. And I watched the cucumbers slowly turning into pickles.

There was an English couple, Geoff and Jean, who were travelling with me and taught me about the operation of the boat. I learned quite a bit about England while talking to them almost every day. Geoff and Jean began by saying, "Why is making pickles while travelling on a boat art?" But they ended up saying, "Maybe it is art. Why not call it art?"

Geoff and Jean encouraged me to eat English cooking every day, making things like sausages and roast beef morning, noon, and night. Gobbling down this food, I got fatter than I had ever been before.

A boat trip and pickles: a slow trip and a slow food. There are places to which you can only travel slowly, and there are things that can only be made slowly.

Arriving in Birmingham, I gave the pickles to friends in Birmingham to eat. The pickles will begin a new journey in people's bodies.'
Shimabuku

nuary 1995,
ity of Kobe
When the earth
were dead and
omeless. Later
n the Hyogo
odern Art picked
station to the
hey documented.

art and cultural
happens it
aphor for the
people. The
Buddhas in
ttention to a
e, while the
useum of
that had become
cidental deaths
h the rubble.

had lost their
from their rails,
ed glass and
on the floor
mortified and
all testified
uch a vicious

Six years later when the evidence of
the institution's destruction was near
impossible to find, the museum was
planning to move to a newly designed
ambitious building on the other side of the
city. To celebrate this "cultural revival from
a natural disaster", they commissioned
artists to make works in relation to the
earthquake and the city's recovery. The
old building was being closed, its future
unsure. The collection was being packed
up and put into temporary storage.
My plan was to re-stage those tableau
moments of devastation that were
photographed that day, carefully using
the real works of art and the now empty
galleries. I wanted to make a fake film
document that bore witness to the horror
of this random cultural destruction and
see how it stood up as metaphor.

The film did not happen for various
reasons, and I have always felt great
sadness about this. Sometimes unrealized
projects come back in a different form, and
I asked the Museum if they would allow
me to publish some of the photographs in
the context of this book so their power
and poignancy could still be shared.'
Tacita Dean

All photographs courtesy Hyogo
Prefectural Museum of Modern Art

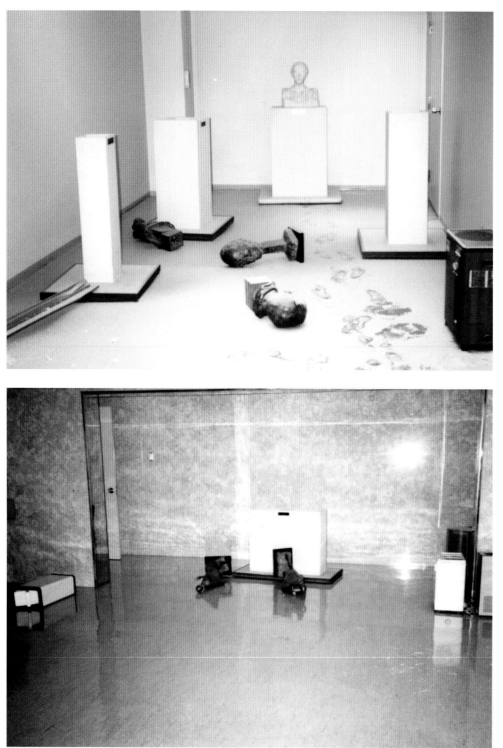

HETEROTOPIAS AND NON-PLACES

Perhaps all this movement blurs our surroundings, like a view from a train window, separating 'us' from 'them'. But is place becoming increasingly dissolved by the developments of the modern world? Is the local vernacular being replaced by international conformity? Are we losing distinct places and places of distinction? Are our most powerful relationships with other places mediated by the screen?

Since the early 1970s, the American artist Allan Sekula has had an enormous influence upon the development of a critically engaged photographic practice, through both his writings and his often large-scale projects that combine photographs and written materials. Contrary to its popular status as a medium of simple veracity, Sekula considers photography a 'fragmentary and incomplete utterance, that is reliant upon its context to provide social significance.' Naturally, as the context changes, so too does the significance of the photographs, something that Sekula has explored in a number of essays or in art works such as *Meditations on a Triptych* (1973–78), in which three family snapshots (the artist's family?) are analysed with an eye to the codes of visual representation, albeit with a full awareness that what the photographs might mean can only ever be established with supplementary information, and even then with no degree of incontestable certainty.

More recently, Sekula has explored a fascination with the sea, and its often missing place in global capitalism. His epic project *Fish Story* (1989–95) explored the movement of manufactured goods in container ships, the hidden bulk of global exchange in a time that speaks more often of electronic instantaneity and the collapse of space. In an extraordinary collection of photographs and texts, Sekula revealed instead the slow and massive movements that lay the foundations of global economics, and the dissolution of place aboard these hulks of ships, most often registered in small countries with few regulations and run by a crew that seldom shares a language. In his more recent *Project for Yokohama*, Sekula gathered various elements – the fish market at Tsukiji, the US naval base and fisheries high school at Yokosuka, and a Frank Gehry-designed fish restaurant in Kobe – and assembled them with an intelligence and delicacy not dissimilar from the sushi chefs he found. The sea is something strange and unknowable to most of us; here it is revealed as a resource for both economics and the military.

'The maritime world is fundamental to late modernity, because it is the cargo container, an American innovation of the 1950s, that makes the global system of manufacture possible…it's a world of gargantuan automation but also of persistent work, of isolated, anonymous hidden work, of great loneliness, displacement and separation from the domestic sphere. For that reason it is interesting to find the social in the sea, as Herman Melville did.'

Allan Sekula

From *Project for Yokohama*

WORKING TITLES 3/31/01 and 6/16/01

No Subs!
Irrational Exuberance (Tsukiji)

WORKING NOTES 3/31/01

The working idea: move between the fish market at Tsukiji, the US naval base and the fisheries high school at Yokosuka, and Frank Gehry's "Fish Dance" restaurant in Kobe. At the Yokohama Archives of History, consider *ukiyo-e* prints depicting the American naval arrival in the 1850s.

From email to Shinji Kohmoto, 3/31/01:

…among the "external" materials for the vitrine at the history archives would be these:

Japanese and English editions of *Kani Kosen* (*The Factory Ship*) by Takiji Kobayashi. I need two copies of the English edition (U. of Tokyo Press, 1973) to show both the cover and the very moving end-paper portrait of Kobayashi. I assume the Tsukiji police station where he was beaten to death in 1933 was destroyed in the fire-bombings and has since been rebuilt or relocated, but my plan for now is to see if it can be filmed or photographed in an evocative way….

Also, the best-selling *manga On War* by Yoshinori Kobayashi. Can we get a publicity photograph of the author? Suppose we approach his publisher, saying I am writing a review of his book, which in a sense is true? I am interested in the physiognomic differences between the two men, the gaunt novelist and the cartoonist-dandy. What I am imagining here is a dialogue between the dead leftist from the 30s and the contemporary rightist. How is the collision of the US submarine with the Japanese fisheries training ship to be read?

PRAYER FOR THE AMERICANS AND THEIR ALLIES 6/16/01

The sky will be our shield
The market will never fall
The icecaps will never melt
And the sea will never be exhausted

From *Project for Yokohama*

From Notebook 5/31/01

Frank Gehry's debt to Japan. *Sushi* architecture. It's not the "vitalism" of the fish (see Kurt Forster on Gehry), but the impeccable decorative arrangement of morsels. Culinary architecture.

Japanese transformations:

morsel, "building block"
[from sea to Tsukiji, from Tsukiji to your mouth]
"Nature" –-{
cartoon, "super-flat"
[subs in toyland]

The *Ehime Maru* cut/sliced by submarine: the *knife ship*. But Gehry's Fish Dance seems so innocent and playful, cartoon-like: a gift from the Good American, leaping upward joyfully.

From Notebook 6/5/01

W observes that everyone in Japan belongs to the same social class.
X confesses to "liking" Yoshinori Kobayashi's right-wing *manga On War*.
Y remarks of Takiji Kobayashi: "No one is interested in the proletarian novel now."
Z comments that there is now no useful distinction to be made between the right and the left.

The American sonar specialist laments: "I miss the Cold War. I didn't want it to end."

Many artists have worked in what we might term a serial manner – one might recall Cézanne's paintings of Mont Saint-Victoire, for example, or Monet's series of haystacks, or the façade of Rouen cathedral – but seldom does the subject matter of the series suggest such an approach. However, this is the case with Yvan Salomone's extraordinary series of watercolour paintings of container ports. The guidelines within which Salomone works are simple, and self-imposed: one painting per week, no more nor less; each painting to be based upon a photograph taken by the artist at the port, whether St Malo (where he was born and continues to live), Shanghai or Rotterdam; all paintings are to be the same format and size, 104 x 145 cm; and no human figures or sudden movements are to be represented.

Perhaps these guidelines – and the degree of repetition they suggest – derive from the subject matter itself. The container ports with which Salomone is fascinated also operate by means of a standardized form, the rigid steel container, the loading, transportation and unloading of which is perhaps the most important part of world trade. Indeed, it is the standardization of the container's form that allows it to be used so widely, and thereby carry such an extraordinary range of items; Salomone's project is perhaps more limited by comparison, the painting of bold architectural forms, and of boats and containers found at the ports he visits, but nevertheless there is much variety to be found within his adopted guidelines. Perhaps what is most striking about the work, however, is the medium in which it is made, and the very handling of it. The use of watercolour for such marine subject matter is perhaps not so unusual – one finds such works, of less industrial settings perhaps, in most coastal towns and cities – but Salomone's use of the medium is quite unique, with flat, almost graphic blocks of colour filling out the heavy forms of the scene, rather than the delicate build-up of shades one might expect. There remains an immense liquidity to the work, however, with water stains over its surfaces, indeed upon the surface of the image, which seems to exist in a process of perpetual 'drying-out'. These are works as much about the flow of colour, form and meaning as the flow of goods and commodities, of the instability of the world around us and all that we can see.

'It is impossible to make an image of a grain silo if I haven't been there.'
Yvan Salomone

opposite, top left
0336. 3. 1099 [blocsusbloc]
Yvan Salomone, 1999

opposite, centre left
0392. 5. 0301 [zwangsideen]
Yvan Salomone

opposite, bottom left
0357. 4. 0400 [portbaniger]
Yvan Salomone, 2000

opposite, top right
0362. 2. 0600 [colimassive]
Yvan Salomone, 2000

opposite, centre right
0397. 2. 0501 [stimmestumm]
Yvan Salomone, 2001

opposite, bottom right
0375. 1. 1100 [cyndycrawfo]
Yvan Salomone, 2000

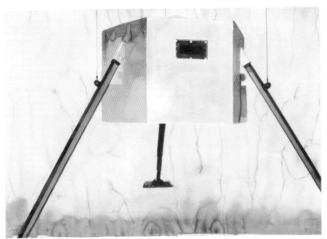 

The Swiss artists Peter Fischli and David Weiss have
worked collaboratively since 1979, producing an
enormous variety of works in many different media,
many of which betray an ongoing fascination with the
beauty and mystery of the everyday. Following the
production of their epic video work *Der Lauf der Dinge*
(The Way Things Go, 1985–87) – a seemingly
seamless chain reaction of explosions and collapses
that necessitated many months of patient preparation –
the artists began work on a series of photographs far
removed from the obsessive studio practice with which
they had previously been engaged. The photographs
of airports, taken on their travels to exhibitions and
elsewhere, at first appear perfectly banal; indeed, the
film-maker John Waters described them as 'mediocre,
glossy, postcard-style photos of exteriors of nondescript
airports' that were, nonetheless, 'absolutely worthy of a
second look'. This is something that is often overlooked
in any consideration of the pictures: that they often
possess a significant formal beauty and an almost
classical (perhaps baroque would be more appropriate)
sense of compositional balance. Here the pattern of
identical tail-fins might create an irresistible visual
rhythm, a fuselage may glow against a bruised and
threatening sky, or those strangely shaped trucks may
perform their arcs around ground staff with a certain
dumpy grace, their movements choreographed by
painted traces upon the glistening tarmac. As Waters
confirms, the viewer of this and much of Fischli and
Weiss's work has 'glimpsed a new kind of 1990s
beauty, over and above the banality of pop or the
exasperation of minimalism into a shockingly tedious,
fair-to-middling, nothing-to-write-home-about, new
kind of masterpiece.'

top left
Untitled
Peter Fischli / David Weiss, 1998 / 2000

middle left
Untitled (Berlin Tegel)
Peter Fischli / David Weiss, 1991 / 1992

bottom left
Untitled (Tokyo)
Peter Fischli / David Weiss, 1990 / 2003

top right
Untitled
Peter Fischli / David Weiss, 1988 / 2000

middle right
Untitled (Rio Air France Jumbo)
Peter Fischli / David Weiss, 1989 / 1998

bottom right
Untitled (Amsterdam Esso)
Peter Fischli / David Weiss, 1998 / 2000

170 ROOM EIGHT Heterotopias and Non-places

'I suspect that the airport will be the true city of the 21st century. The great airports of the planet are already the suburbs of an invisible world capital, a virtual metropolis whose faubourgs are named Heathrow, Kennedy, Charles de Gaulle, Nagoya, a centripetal city whose population forever circles its notional centre, and will never need to gain access to its dark heart.'
J. G. Ballard

'I noted the features of this silent world: the memory erasing white architecture; the enforced leisure that fossilized the nervous system; ...the apparent absence of an social structure; the timelessness of a world beyond boredom, with no past, no future and a diminishing present. Perhaps this was what a leisure-dominated future would resemble? Nothing could ever happen in this affectless realm, where entropic drift calmed the surfaces of a thousand swimming pools.'

J. G. Ballard

Since 1996, the English artist Stephen Hughes has been making photographs of places that seem to be on the edge. They might be on the edge of the coast, the zone along which the elements of land and sea make their twice-daily territorial claims; or they might be on the edges of the city, beneath or along the arterial routes that speed the urban into the rural. A half-built holiday resort, a desolate lorry park or an equally empty airport – these are transient places whose surfaces seem to bear the markings of time, yet upon which memory seems unable to cling. That is not to say that they lack atmosphere, however; these are places in which desperation and *ennui* provoke one another in tides of emotional advancement and retreat.

These are transitory spaces in a more fundamental sense too; not only do they disperse people or vehicles elsewhere, but they also seem to disperse themselves. These are entropic spaces, and it is Hughes's notable achievement that he has been able to find a sense of form in places whose form is dissipating, and he has done so without the need of imposing a compositional framework. These are landscapes whose elements seem to have drifted together momentarily and, with the fall of the tide or the lifting of the mist, will drift apart once more.

top left
South of Estepona
Stephen Hughes, 1999

Malaga 1, Spain
Stephen Hughes, 1999

top right
Famara, Lanzarote
Stephen Hughes, 1999

Swanley, England
Stephen Hughes, 1997

ROOM EIGHT Heterotopias and Non-places 173

For over thirty years now, Boris Mikhailov has worked on numerous series of photographs, each of which explores the place of the individual within a public ideology: first communism, and then its collapse into capitalism, in his native Ukraine; more recently, the uneasy relationship between these two systems in Berlin, where he now lives. The nature of the projects might change, as might their sense of scale, from the intimate *Crimean Snobbery* (1982), to the epic tragedy of *Case History* (1999), yet in all of them we can find the same concerns, as noted by the critic Lech Lechowicz: 'the past, relation to tradition, recent and long gone, the relation between what is social and what is personal, the sphere of the public and the sphere of the intimate.'

Restricted from travelling from his birth-town for much of his adult life, Mikhailov has acknowledged the power that this bleak industrial city has had upon him: 'Kharkov is my place in a very real sense. I think the West has too many distractions that can be a hindrance to my work.' Now resident in the West, these 'distractions', far from hindering his work, have actually become a part of it. In *TV-Mania*, Mikhailov turns his camera upon the world as it is represented on European satellite television. The subjects that catch his attention are familiar from his earlier works, the great themes of art themselves – life, death, love, power and sex – yet here our relationship to them is ambivalent. A screaming newborn, a missile trail, mating rhinos, a shelled apartment block, late-night Italian erotica – the mediated world is made proximate while continuing to retain its distance.

*from **TV-Mania** series*
Boris Mikhailov, 1991–2002

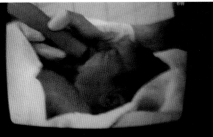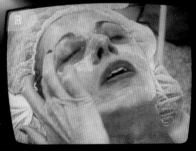

from **TV-Mania** *series*
Boris Mikhailov, 1991–2002

POSTSCRIPT

So I'm sitting here trying best to describe 'place'.
Do I describe where I am?
Do I say I'm looking out over the corrugated iron roof of my
studio in the centre of Berlin, in what was once a railway
storage building that sits nearly next to the canal that
famously divided this city in half?
Do I describe the weather, the birdlife, the smell?
I have realized in my search for a description of place, it is
so often best imagined through the senses and through the
memory of the senses. If I were to go east now, soon the air
would smell of the cheap brown coal that for me is the
place that was the GDR. I did not know the GDR, except
for one daytrip there in 1987, but that doesn't prevent me
from imagining the place, remembering the place – on
account of that smell. And now I hear a magpie, and the
crows and the swallows. Everything is a bit quieter so I can
hear further – cars and the wind in the trees and a plane far
off. Something about the combination of sounds tells me it
is early evening and that the sun is out and it is summer.
Place connecting with time.

I played with many ideas about place for this book but in
the end I realized it can only ever be personal. Place can
never be generalized like it is on the Euro notes; it will
always connect to somewhere in our autobiographies –
future and past. It is an amorphous ungainly feeling
that enables us to articulate feelings of familiarity or
estrangement, and for the most part it is better left
ignored because it can be unbearable.

So I tried to imagine how best to describe place and
thought of this poem written by W. S. Graham after his
friend Peter Lanyon was killed gliding over West Penwith
in Cornwall. I cannot read it without experiencing the
amalgam of feelings that connect me to that place.
The description of place will always reside in the detail.

Tacita Dean

THE THERMAL STAIR

For the painter Peter Lanyon killed in a gliding
accident 1964

I called today, Peter, and you were away.
I look out over Botallack and over Ding
Dong and Levant and over the jasper sea.

Find me a thermal to speak and soar to you from
Over Lanyon Quoit and the circling stones standing
High on the moor over Gurnard's Head where some

Time three foxglove summers ago, you came.
The days are shortening over Little Parc Owles.
The poet or painter steers his life to maim

Himself somehow for the job. His job is Love
Imagined into words or paint to make
An object that will stand and will not move.

Peter, I called and you were away, speaking
Only through what you made and at your best.
Look, there above Botallack, the buzzard riding

The salt updraught slides off the broken air
And out of sight to quarter a new place.
The Celtic sea, the Methodist sea is there.

    You said once in the Engine
    House below Morvah
    That words make their world
    In the same way as the painter's
    Mark surprises him
    Into seeing new.
    Sit here on the sparstone
    In this ruin where
    Once the early beam
    Engine pounded and broke
    The air with industry.

Now the chuck of daws
And the listening sea.

"Shall we go down" you said
"Before the light goes
And stand under the old
Tinworkings around
Morvah and St Just?"
You said "Here is the sea
Made by alfred wallis
Or any poet or painter's
Eye it encountered.
Or is it better made
By all those vesselled men
Sometime it maintained?
We all make it again."

Give me your hand, Peter,
To steady me on the word.

Seventy-two by sixty,
Italy hangs on the wall.
A woman stands with a drink
In some polite place
And looks at SARACINESCO
And turns to mention space.
That one if she could
Would ride Artistically
The thermals you once rode.

Peter, the phallic boys
Begin to wink their lights.
Godrevy and the Wolf
Are calling Opening Time.
We'll take the quickest way
The tin singers made.
Climb here where the hand
Will not grasp on air.
And that dark-suited man
Has set the dominoes out
On the Queen's table.
Peter, we'll sit and drink
And go in the sea's roar

To Labrador with wallis
Or rise on Lanyon's stair.

Uneasy, lovable man, give me your painting
Hand to steady me taking the word-road home.
Lanyon, why is it you're earlier away?
Remember me wherever you listen from.
Lanyon, dingdong dingdong from carn to carn.
It seems tonight all Closing bells are tolling
Across the Duchy shire wherever I turn.

W. S. Graham

TALK

Tacita Dean, Joseph L. Koerner, Jeremy Millar, Simon Schama

TALK

Tacita Dean is an artist based in Berlin and London.
Joseph L. Koerner is an art historian at the Courtauld Institute of Art, London.
Jeremy Millar is an artist, writer and curator based in Whitstable, Kent.
Simon Schama is a writer, broadcaster and professor of art history at Columbia University, New York.

JM: The question with which I want to start is simply what is place? What does place mean to you?

JK: I guess I could start with an anecdote. My father was a painter and he used to drag us around to views he wanted to paint, views that were significant to him because they had to do with his returning to Vienna as a Jew and finding a 'place' again. Now, I would always try to find a spot in whatever he was painting so that I could paint it myself. But one time I rebelled and decided to turn away from his view and look some place else. All of a sudden, the world looked completely without organization and interest. I produced the most horrible picture.

SS: How old were you?

JK: I must have been about twelve.

SS: How to become a modernist…it's all about unframing.

JK: Unframing, exactly. It's all about knowing what *a place* looks like…I mean the way we've learned to *know* that we're in a place, as opposed to being not in a place (that is, not in a framed view). I guess where I had turned towards wasn't a place.

SS: In television, I worry about how you can ever get away from this kind of framing. You can try to get away from the painter's frame, but you simply surrender yourself to another: the camera's frame. We have this argument between film and video, where videomakers claim transparency, claim the integrity of some sort of transparent spontaneity. They claim a kind of dumbness, claim that the camera sees by itself. But of course it's not like that; it's almost impossible not to compose something when you set up your slice of space. Do you think that one can ever escape from some sort of framing?

JK: No, probably not.

SS: To be boundary-less.

JK: When I bring students in front of a painting, by Claude Lorrain, for example, we try to determine what a framed view is. It's a kind of Holy Grail – one assumes that the framed view is what one is either getting at or getting away from. An early nineteenth-century painting, for example, puts the frame slightly off-centre.

SS: But dislodging it isn't the same thing as getting rid of it, is it?

JK: No. But do you think there really is this desire to not have a framed view? Isn't that disorientating?

SS: Oh, a very good question. It was Auden who talked about disorientation. It was in a lecture when he was speaking about the trait of always comparing deserts and oceans. Sometimes people who are lost at sea, because the eye doesn't work properly, find themselves thinking of shifting sand. And often people talk about the desert in oceanic terms – camels are 'ships of the desert', for example, and so on. When I was doing the BBC films of my book *Landscape and Memory*, I snuck one in about the sea. I was so struck by the kind of repulsion that writers in antiquity had felt for it. The sense of being in deep oceanic space was literally repellent for them. It was where they thought monsters lay, and these monsters were often of their own imaginings. Our own version of that is 'Space

Oddity', with David Bowie being lost out there, somewhere out there. I think it's actually a primal terror we all have. We start *in utero*, in a place that seems to have comforting boundaries and we swish around in there, knowing what we know. But then there is this space–place distinction, and space is much scarier because it's harder to graph.

JK: Do you suppose that the modern desire, if it's an index of modernity, not to place oneself into a preframed view – into someone else's experience – but to actually *have* one's own experience, one's own frame, is because there is an oceanic sense of endlessly framed character on the landscape?

SS: Well, I think about Mondrian's *Pier and Ocean*. Through half-closed eyes, Mondrian sees the light glinting off that jetty and it resolves itself as a kind of route to metaphysical nowhereness. For him it becomes abstraction, and that abstraction turns out to look like a grid.

TD: It's like longitude and latitude and time.

JM: Something that Deleuze and Guattari talk about is the ocean as a space which had traditionally been considered as very smooth and indeterminate and shapeless, but which, with the grids of longitude and latitude, becomes a sort of sharp geometric space. Space is made knowable and predictable to some extent.

TD: But then, if you're in this shifting mass of grey for days and days on end, the human relationship to those grids is actually no relationship at all. And what's more, those grids are also entirely to do with time, in the sense that you have to have a clock to understand them. If the clock goes wrong then you're back to…well, I was going to say square one, but it's actually a pre-grid experience.

SS: Yes, some sort of primal incoherence. I think that one accepts, I suppose instinctively, the inevitability of framing. My own framing is very often temporal. Some of the obsessions in *Landscape and Memory* are all about the attempts in different human cultures to nail down places in the historical continuum so that they become identified

through a kind of mythic experience. In reality, of course, these shift, disappear, reform, and deconstruct themselves. The German forest is a good case in point: it's not there any more. It's one of those places that are artificially preserved in memory as places to go to, or places to point at, so that people can orientate themselves for a particular purpose in a moment of shared national communion, either for good or ill. Take Glastonbury, for example.

We start *in utero*, in a place that seems to have comforting boundaries and we swish around in there, knowing what we know

JK: An interesting device in sixteenth-century landscapes is the relationship between a view and a milestone. Early landscape artists – instinctively, I think – include milestones in their landscapes. Similarly, Brueghel will have either a cross or a something that is prior to the view but by which the view constitutes itself. So there's a relationship to marking and framing that early on.

SS: But the milestones, do they have legible figures on them?

JK: Actually, they don't.

SS: Right, it's a pre-mensurated world isn't it really, if that's a word.

JK: It's not unlike the Romantic shorthand of the wanderer coming across a stone and having a kind of descriptive relationship to it, like in a Wordsworth poem. The landscape's already built as a place that's marked.

SS: And often paintings have tiny churches on the horizons. One thinks casually that they are meant as a vanishing point, but they aren't always. They are actually rather arbitrarily put in. But it means that the horizon – the landscape – has a point of salvation, indicated by the puncture of the spire. It's a meaningful gesture, rather than a formal one.

TD: You know with Robert Smithson's *Spiral Jetty* in Utah there's a hidden rock in the nearby landscape, and if you find it you can see that it's the sightline for the jetty.

SS: When the jetty started to disappear, there was a big debate for years and years about whether to save it or not. It was said 'Oh well, fine, that's mutability.'

TD: But Smithson didn't want it to disappear. He was very clear about that. I'm sure he'd be delighted that it's reappeared. It's like his *Partially Buried Woodshed*. He wrote a whole paper for the art school where it's installed that they had to preserve it. It's destroyed now.

SS: I think he had a very strong monumental streak in him; it wasn't all about passage and change, like he claimed. There are some artists who talk about happenstance in the most disingenuous way. It's like Francis Bacon – sorry to get off 'place' for a bit – always said that he worked spontaneously, while not mentioning his 9,000 study drawings. I just don't believe Smithson when he says 'Here I am wandering through a landscape and that's just

Very often the power or the impotence of a place in the public and historical imagination is defined by access

fine, it's chewed up, I'm going to chew it up a bit more. Bring in the truck.'

JM: That leads nicely onto my next question. Is place fixed and if not in what ways do you think it's changed historically?

SS: In *Spiral Jetty*, but in America in general, there's this weird, complicated relationship between transience and historical markers. I mean as a nation it's very keen on its historical markers: Gettysburg, Mount Rushmore and so on.

John Brinckerhoff Jackson, who wrote about the cultural meaning of the American landscape, was great about how roads and routes to and away swallow things up by making places more accessible. Very often the power or the impotence of a place in the public and historical imagination is defined by access. It's always amazing to me when I fly over America, as someone who is still very bewitched by the American landscape – pure land, but not pure – that other people are completely indifferent to what they see out of the window. Fifteen years ago, pilots used to love doing their little spiel about 'On your right there's Lake Erie, on your left is the Grand Canyon.' They never do it any more. Instead they now say 'In two minutes, your Tom Hanks movie will be starting and we will serve you your congealed omelette.' I was sitting next to a Russian the first time I flew over the continental divide. He was doubly thunderstruck by (a) what he was seeing and (b) that no one seemed to care.

JK: That's also expressed in Am-Trak trains, which are unimaginable from a European point of view – the windows are up here….

SS: Huge.

JK: …but completely filthy, and no one looks out of them. There is no sense of actually experiencing anything except being in a state of transit.

SS: The archaeology of that in the 1930s was completely different. I think it was Walter Benjamin who said 'You often see landscape through a kind of flicker of a car window, which is sort of like a celluloid frame.' I think much was made of that in the thirties. I always remember that beautiful moment in *North by Northwest* when Cary Grant's sitting in the train and it's pulling out and going somewhere north and west from Grand Central, and then you're up in the Finger Lakes or somewhere. It's intensely important that you're seeing that. In fact, it is a film about place, isn't it? You end up at Mount Rushmore, but it's important to have those lakes slide past in the falling light. There must be many films in the thirties where the observation car is part of the landscape.

JK: In 1989 when the Berlin Wall fell, I decided to bike through Germany from the Baltic coast through Berlin down to Prague. Since there were no normal maps you could buy for East Germany, I went to the Harvard map collection and xeroxed old pre-Second World War maps and then made a route (my high-school thinking that this would be a perfectly reasonable thing to do). But when I got there I found that the small roads between towns just give up at certain points. While I was travelling, and long afterwards, I heard rumours that permission had been required for internal travel in the GDR – even for its citizens. These rumors turned out to be false, part of a mythology of the old regime's strangeness. But these focused in me a feeling of moving about a forbidden geography. In the interstices between towns the roads had grown over, completely seeded with bushes and trees.

Modern myths about place change when we move from a situation of rootedness to one of itinerancy

When you'd get to the top of a hill it was a forest, and the experience was one of a…of an enormous variety, a glorious variety of road surfaces. You'd start off with these big slabs of concrete with metal bolts (which they specialized in), and then the concrete slabs would become less and less, and then it would be a row of overgrown concrete slabs, until finally it became just bushes. And so at the point at which it's only bushes and you've lost the road, we would crawl over the hill, carrying the bikes on our shoulders, hoping that the road would eventually show up again and all of a sudden the road would begin to reappear and finally you were able to plant the bike down and coast into these towns from a direction that no visitor, at that point, had ever come from. So there was a kind of feeling like, in those early anthropological descriptions that Claude Lévi-Strauss talks about in *Tristes Tropiques*, of coming to a village for the first time, but from the rear, sort of through the backdoor of a cultural landscape that had been overgrown by nature. And that's the sort of landscape that I find very interesting. It's very, very frightening but the whole

of the north-east of the United States is in a way a much older version of that. If you go to Vermont and New Hampshire, what one finds is not what you would think when you go there: pure nature, with big rocks and boulders. In fact it's an overgrown, very heavily transformed agricultural landscape that lost its economic viability years ago and so it's criss-crossed with paths and cemeteries. One has a sense, walking through there, of the natural world reconquering these cultural landscapes, and so it's a sort of inverse of the myth of the first encounter.

TD: So in a way that relates to your question on whether it's a specific place, although of course place changes the whole time. But whether or not the notion of place itself has changed as much is more difficult to work out.

JK: Certainly all narratives about place change over time. I see you have the Edward Casey book *The Fate of Place*, which explains very well how modern myths about place change when we move from a situation of rootedness to one of itinerancy. When human society was rooted, we didn't have a sense of a place as being a place, because anything that wasn't that place wasn't in the world. It was unimaginable to move beyond whatever one knew. I often wonder whether people have always been troubled by the same anonymity and situatedness that we now feel, and whether it really is such a deeply modern concern or just a modern expression of a historical experience. Certainly, the first articulations of it are in the form of landscape painting. I think I could write the same story about early sixteenth-century landscape as I could about romantic landscape: urban dwellers looking suddenly from an itinerant perspective at a rural or agricultural economy to which they didn't belong. So is that the perennial story of representation of place?

TD: I think it's with the advent of linear perspective, where for the first time artists actually depict *space*, that place is created. Because you create a stable or you create a house and then the relationship between the two, between the background and the foreground, becomes apparent…you then begin to see a bit of countryside and that becomes identifiable as a place, rather than just merely space. You lose the gold backgrounds, and you start creating what we define as places, a church or whatever. And then, over two hundred years or so, the idea of place becomes more and more identifiable.

JK: That's absolutely the evil moment for anti-modernists. Heidegger is clear on this in his essay on the age of the world picture, which basically describes the condition of the world as a representation. All of a sudden you reach the modern state, which is a condition in which the world appears, as you put it, as a place, through a representation that's coordinated and coherent by a positioning of points of view within a kind of grid. And I suppose the question would be, does pictorial representation have that great an effect on people? That is, did people who lived in an era in which paintings were painted with gold backgrounds actually experience themselves as living in that world picture? That's the assumption of both the modernist and anti-modernist arguments. They are either for or against that perspectival picture. But is the perspectival picture really the thing in which people started to live? I guess the difficulty of imagining pre-modern space, though, is that it's never going to be represented. That is, by definition it's just beyond the limits of what's represented. I think you might find it where the Virgin and Child have been plucked out of a composition that was fundamentally rooted in their presence – as the *place* of the picture – but since the picture's 'place' is the Virgin's and Child's bodies, if you pluck them out, you suddenly have something different, something before perspective, or even without perspective, a sense of space free of a coordinate system.

TD: Gold space.

JK: Gold space indeed. The early sixteenth-century German artist Albrecht Altdorfer painted paradigmatic miracle-working images of the Virgin, some of the most ecstatic miracles of the Virgin. In his home town of Regensburg, he was the great impresario of this image cult. But he was also the first person in western art to take away the Virgin and Child and paint the residue. Some say these are first true landscape paintings.

SS: I think that the successful breakthrough of three dimensions in the Renaissance, as a device for controlling space, actually works against the idea of place. You can trap space brilliantly, or extend it, but it also means that the world is reduced to a set of controllable spaces. So it's ambiguous. I mean it's the moment when Europeans discover other people's places, especially sacred places,

> You can trap space brilliantly, or extend it, but it also means that the world is reduced to a set of controllable spaces

as points of pilgrimage and deposits of memory. Mexico City had been a place with its own geographical logic. And it then comes under the Spanish grid, which is a control device.

TD: But then, what kind of culture hasn't done that, except for nomadic people?

SS: But it is possible for empires, like the British in India, to more or less keep other people's places the way they are and then make their own separate places, which are kinds of European compounds and which keep the other cultures....

TD: Out.

SS: Out. Yes, exactly.

JM: But what about those cultures that try to control others by creating separate places within their *own* place?

SS: Like what?

JM: I'm thinking of the Jewish ghettos in Venice, for instance.

SS: That's a good question, isn't it? Well, weirdly the horror of that is that there's an attempt to create a kind of self-imploding void but actually all it does is create a stronger sense of place, for both those inside and outside the ghetto. The synagogues get closer and closer and the butchers' shops and the peoples' dwellings and get more and more crowded and conglomerate. Everything one reads about Lodz or Krakow or Warsaw or anywhere was that they remained in that sense an 'experience space'. They experienced place as kind of resistance to what was facing them.

JM: And the irony is that in Israel today you get the similar experience but it's the Palestinians' experience, that kind of ghettoization, because they're controlled.

SS: Well, that's true in their towns. But I don't think the settler compounds are places at all. They're just kind of portable suburbs. They are the suburban lawned barracks with narrow corridors of heavily patrolled security for people to commute to Jerusalem or wherever. They're complete Nowhere-villes. It's very weird because they were created by people who absolutely invoke place as the entitlement to do that.

TD: But to go back briefly to our discussion about linear perspective, we have to remember the importance of heaven as a place, which of course we've lost now. And I was going to make that point when Simon was talking about aeroplanes. They have screwed up our perspective on everything because now we're looking down on Earth, a perspective we never had. It used to be God's alone.

JK: It's mysterious how painters actually produce these high views. Before the advent of the aeroplane, where did they actually get the world picture as such? People, of course, loved going up high towers to get that kind of prospect. But you have a lot of these amazing views before you have high towers. The other good question, I suppose, which goes along with the idea of moving and not moving that Simon was referring to before, is why do we always assume that place is only accessible visually? I was just reading this wonderful anthropologist of art, Alfred Gell, who died very young. He argued that people conceived of demons, for example, aurally rather than visually. The idea of having visual evidence for whether or not they actually *saw*

demons is completely secondary. So this discussion of perspectival space, itinerant space, like whether we have windows in railroads, is only part of it. What about things like smell? To me, Austria, where I have my strongest feeling of place, is all about opening the door to late nineteenth-century apartment buildings and smelling a mixture of plaster and boiled cabbage. That to me means I'm in Austria. I mean I could see a film and think 'that looks a little like Austria', but it's not boiled cabbage and….

TD: Well with some of the artists we're featuring, there are one or two who work with place through sound, like Janet Cardiff, for example. She describes a place entirely aurally, but smell with visual art is a tricky one.

JK: Right, it's one of those dead ends.

TD: Actually I have tried to do it. There's a smell factory in Ashford in Kent and I wanted to give them a piece of tarred wood that smelled exactly like the *Cutty Sark* and have them turn it into a sort of a tincture of the essence of the *Cutty Sark*. But I haven't managed to pull that one off.

JM: Do you think that space is something that is more abstract and unknowable, and place is something that is

Is it possible to experience space, or can we experience place but only imagine space?

more corporeal…I'm just wondering whether it's possible to experience space, or whether we can experience place but only imagine space?

JK: One terminological issue, which seems to me at once banal and interesting, is that theorists of space and place often use the terms in reverse mode. Michel de Certeau, whom I like very much, is a theorist of space who has an inverted view of which is which. One person might think that place is a pre-modern condition of rootedness, 'Here I am on this spot', but for another it's space that is grid and so forth. I suppose, it seems to me that from some broader, more philosophical, perspective, the one probably exists nestled in the other. That is, you can't imagine the node of being there in that spot except within some representation of it, that is, within a sense of place. I guess what I mean is that I find myself contesting the story that we move from place to space.

Maybe we experience place but only recognize space? Can you recognize space without experiencing it?

TD: But maybe we experience place but only recognize space? You can recognize space without experiencing it, can't you? It's a different kind of action or activity.

JK: Yes, well the question of experience is something that's fascinated me. It's the structure, place as a structure of experience, or experience as fundamentally having a spatial structure to it. The condition of modernity is having experiences that no one else has had, and that experience is a thing, like a commodity, that is there, out there, waiting for you. The relationship between the experienced world and the act of experiencing, if I can say it that way, has a spatial structure, and that spatial structure has, as one of its climaxes, a sense that *this* is a place, just like *this* is an experience. I mean if it's pared down to its basic story, it seems to me, one moves along and then all of a sudden one is aware of something that is more than just moving along and existing, something meaningful. I don't know if that is 'an experience' or 'a place', or if the two go hand in hand. But with both we do ask ourselves 'Can I have one? What is it? Do I know it when I see it?'

JM: What do you think the effect of digital communication technology has been on a sense of place?

JK: There's an installation by an artist called Ken Goldberg, who is a robotics expert. He has made a garden in a technology museum in Linz in Austria. It's a little garden about the size of a table, and it's watered, seeded and tended by the community of people who log on to its website from all over the world and observe it through a webcam. You can squirt tiny bits of water, and if you've done 100 hits you're allowed to put a seed in. It's all about distance and the Garden of Eden and so forth, but the artist has conceived of it as a very clear, if even almost slightly banal, critique, a critical gesture, that is. I'd imagine that the *last* thing that a person would want to do would be to garden on the web, because even if they didn't have a real garden they could turn their chair, open their window and plant seeds in a window box. The amount of effort and energy that goes into logging on in order to do it is comparatively huge – you have to get your personal PIN number, you have to take hours to do it, and so forth – but, contrary to what the artist imagined, people love it. They're very, very obsessed with it. But one of the two things that people worry about is that, of course, there's no proof for the person logged onto the website and sitting in their bedroom that the garden actually exists, because it could be just a film loop.

TD: Surely the seeds will grow?

JK: Yes, the seeds will grow and one can sort of follow that, but the whole thing could be preprogrammed. You might not have put the seeds in yourself. It might be that you have just pressed a button and there are hundreds of other people doing the same, and then there's a film of geranium seed being planted, and you then go back and watch the film of it growing and it's all computer-

Once the High Street loses its specificity, everything that we as non-nomadic peoples expect of our social centres will have changed

programmed. So one anxiety is that the garden doesn't exist, but the other, which is even stronger, is that visitors to the museum in Linz don't believe that the camera arm and the watering system is being manipulated by people on the web. That seems completely implausible. But is it really? Why can't people thousands of miles away have a relationship with this garden? They're doing stuff with the world, they're making little clicks. To say that they're far away from the garden and so therefore can't be controlling it is to have a strong belief that life is made out of organic materials and soil, as opposed to plastic and glass and a screen. I mean we have all sorts of ideological prejudices about what are good materials and bad. It seems to me to go back to all sorts of debates about soil versus itinerancy, and issues that became political in the thirties – what it means to be a people who doesn't have a garden, for instance, which was the critique of Jews in Germany. One of the fascinating features of the great book on perspective by Erwin Panofsky, *Perspective as Symbolic Form*, is that it's not about the hegemony of the western idea of the situated observer, all powerful all over the world, but rather a vindication of a relationship to the world that doesn't actually have to be rooted in mud and soil.

JM: There was another question I wanted to ask you which, again, relates to this. It's about globalization and place. Do you think that place has become and will become more important, culturally and politically, as a result of globalization?

JK: I guess what I would say is that in some obvious areas of western cosmopolitan existence the experience of what we think are the effects of globalization reflect the same narrative as all the other anxieties about modernity. It's just another version of the same story. One example is that now, instead of the old, wonderful espresso store with the man who makes his own bread with his own hands and has a few slabs of extremely good prosciutto ham on top, we have Starbucks and no ham or man with mud on his boots. All of a sudden one High Street looks exactly the same in one part of the town as it does in another, and the same in different towns. The High Street equals market equals the *agora*, which is the place that constitutes a city. Once it loses its specificity, everything that we as non-nomadic peoples expect of our social centres will have changed.

Of course, how those changes will affect people will be very different in parts of the world where eighteenth- and nineteenth-century urban hubs are being replaced compared with agricultural economies. What's interesting is that we always talk about globalization as involving some kind of loss, and it seems that this loss is to do with place, that the yearning with which all of us are filled is a yearning for place, a place where one is. But actually globalization itself is caused or impelled by a sense of place: I'm sure that it comes about because of staggering boredom with the countryside. The experience of the city is partly an experience of wanting change, and romantic ideas of the countryside come from a condition of being allergic to change.

JM: It's retrospective, of course, the countryside being invented after cities are built, and then only when people who live in cities start to visit it and think of it as the countryside – even if those people once lived there or their parents still do. Without going to another place, one doesn't think about one's own location as a place.

JK: Absolutely not.

TD: But that touches on how you say memory defines a place so that the place no longer exists, just a memory of it,

The countryside is invented after cities are built, and then only when people who live in cities start to visit it

and what's really interesting and the most impossible thing about this subject is that you can never really put your finger on it. It's so amorphous. It's something that we all think we understand but don't really. We understand it emotionally, I think, but we don't really understand it cerebrally, like we understand space.

SS: Talking about the homogenization of the street and memory, I remember when Petty Cury in Cambridge was an old Victorian street with a few palms. Not that I'm not nostalgic or romantic about it – it was scruffy and mostly smelt of piss – but what replaced it was a pedestrianized street, and there were all these sort of quasi-medieval shop signs which said 'Boots' and 'Hardy's' and 'Courts', and so on.

We understand place emotionally, but we don't really understand it cerebrally, like we understand space

TD: Just like Canterbury.

SS: Very much like Canterbury.

TD: Have you ever seen *A Canterbury Tale*, the Michael Powell film? It opens in the bombed-out Canterbury and you can just see signs sticking up out of the rubble saying 'Boots was here'. I was born there, and they've now rebuilt it with all these replica medieval places. They are the most depressing of all. But the film is just a beautiful, beautiful document about a city that has been destroyed. Of course, Berlin is quite extraordinary like that. It's unbelievable to think of the decimation that happened there. You look around now and you can't believe how they could have possibly created a city so quickly from just rubble. It's quite amazing. And there is a hill just made of the rubble. It's like a slag heap, quite near the Olympic stadium.

SS: What's on it?

TD: Nothing. It's just a hill, but it's entirely made of the rubble. It's like that hill in Wiltshire that has this very, very strange quality to it…Silbury Hill. Nobody knows why, but for a lot of people it's very spiritual. One of the artists in the book does corn circles there and people believe in them. But in fact his work is to make the circles and then collect all the documentation.

SS: We shot there once. At West Kennett Longbarrow, which is almost opposite Silbury Hill, there is a long moored, upside-down boat-shaped hill, and then Silbury is

this extraordinary sort of breast-like conical shape. Between them at the back of them are the fields that Spielberg used in *Saving Private Ryan* to represent – this is actually great for your book – to represent the American Midwest. He said there was nowhere in the Midwest that was like the Midwest any more. So in Wiltshire, where I actually live, you see the fake façade of the house, and there's an American windmill, and the officers are coming to tell Mrs Ryan that her boy's been killed. It's a shot, a huge wide shot, of a car going towards this house and then there's a reverse looking out at what's supposed to be Indiana or North Dakota or something and it's in fact Salisbury. And it completely beggars the imagination. Spielberg clearly, perversely, thought place was transposable and believed that the authenticity of this particular place could be achieved only by actually exporting it, by finding it and devising it and controlling it and re-creating it in Salisbury. The film imagination of moveable place.

TD: But that's what's so beautiful about fiction.

SS: Yes, but he's inadvertently doing it in the place of all places, the place where the landscape is the bearer of all kinds of meaning and memories.

JM: I saw Chris Marker's film *La Jetée* again recently. People always say the film plays with time and memory. But what struck me, while I was watching it, that it's not just playing with memory temporally but spatially as well, and that's conveyed in a way by the title, which in French has a sense of throwing. I mean *La Jetée* comes from the verb *jeter*, to throw, and '*la jetée*' is something that is literally thrown. And the jetty throws you out into the middle of this oceanic space you were talking about earlier as well. I just wonder how memory disorientates spatially.

SS: Well, again, back to my own memories, I grew up near Southend, and Southend pier for me was peopled – it was very much *a place*. It was the last reach of human place out into something that was much trickier. And it was much trickier because of the immense void of mud. I mean it was amazingly undelineated, no clear line between ocean and land, so you could walk for a very long way when the tide was out. It was an amorphous and indeterminate kind of zone, whereas the pier was absolutely part of a populated town – in a way, an extension of the town.

TD: But place doesn't exist without memory, right?

SS: No, it doesn't.

TD: Even if it's a sort of cultural memory or collective or official memory. Like sometimes you sense you've been somewhere when you haven't.

SS: Right. Apparently nostalgia was once diagnosed as a clinical condition. It affected the Swiss, interestingly enough. It was said they were cured by opium leeches and trips back to the Alps. And also the Russians. There are wonderful letters from the eighteenth century in which the Russians say half their regiment had gone down with nostalgia. It was actually typhus or TB, but they actually thought they were clinically incapable of fighting. They were taken back home.

TD: Homesickness.…

SS: Exactly, exactly. And very often the home is absolutely an imagined place or a fictitiously remembered or half-remembered place that people want to exist, but it exists almost entirely in memory.

Often the home is an imagined place or a fictitiously remembered place that exists almost entirely in memory

JM: Something that Joseph said earlier was that just as people ask themselves 'What is an experience? Am I experiencing an experience?', they ask themselves. 'What is place? Am I in a place?' And the tourist is the embodiment of both. I mean when you go on holiday you tell yourself 'I'm in a place now. This is worth visiting.'

TD: Yes, but how is that place defined?

SS: Beaches aren't places. Beaches are non-places, they're definitely a non-site. They're peripheries, yes, and the choice for people is 'Are you a beach person or do you actually want to do things?'

TD: In Germany I've had this conversation with people, 'Are you a sea person or are you a mountain person?' People are really mountainous there. It's really interesting because I would never think for a minute that I was mountainous. I'm definitely sea and it's something to do with the British, well I speak mainly for the English, who are very sea people. What do you crave? Beach or mountain, desert or field?

SS: Well, I'm certainly not mountain. I think for me, having grown up in Essex, the shore at least is a place because of my endless re-experiencing of my childhood memory of playing there and crabs and so on. So it's a defined.…

TD: So beach is a place then, not a non-place?

SS: Well, for most people the beach is just a bestseller and suntan lotion. It is a protection against an immediate experience.

TD: But because you've known the beach as a place, it's always a place for you.

SS: Yes, but it's a hinterland and I would always have to experience that hinterland in order to see the edge of it.

TD: But the mountains, for you, would not be so much of a place?

SS: No, absolutely not.

TD: For me they are a space that I perceive culturally through other people's experiences.

SS: I'm still incredibly impressed by the eighteenth-century English landscapist John Robert Cozens, who in his watercolours of the Alps created an art of mountain disorientation by manipulating perspective in an incredibly self-conscious way in order to flatten distances and to produce alarming relationships between verticals and horizontals.

JM: I'm always interested in the differences between the way that Turner painted and Ruskin drew mountains. Because, even though they were so closely associated, their approach was so very, very different. Ruskin was deliberately trying to create a recognizable place with very precise depiction, whereas Turner created much more impressionistic scenes. He was trying to capture the experience of a place.

SS: Yes. But the fantastic thing about Ruskin is that when he writes about Turner and truth, he berates people for thinking that Turner's art is not literal naturalism and therefore can't be truthful. Even though his own way of drawing a place is to plot it in definable space in the most academic way, when he writes about Turner he's in a kind of froth of almost metaphysical excitement. He's utterly in Turnerland and it frustrates him. He's attacked by a terrible sense of bad faith and doubt that he is unable to convey in his drawing what he loves about Turnerian clouds, skies and boats. It torments him actually that he can't represent what a place means to him.

TD: Life must have been unbearable.

SS: Well, he went mad.

THE ARTISTS

DOUG AITKEN
b. 1968, Redondo Beach, California (USA); lives in Los Angeles (USA)

Select exhibitions
'metallic sleep', Kunstmuseum Wolfsburg; Kunst-Werke, Berlin, 2001
'new ocean, a shifting exhibition', Fondazione Sandretto Re Rebaudengo Per L'Arte, Turin; Kunsthaus Bregenz, Bregenz; Tokyo Opera City Gallery, Tokyo; Serpentine Gallery, London, 2001–3
'rise', Louisiana Museum of Modern Art, Humlebæk, 2002
Kunsthalle Zürich, Zurich, 2003

Select publications
Doug Aitken and Dean Kuipers, *I am a Bullet. Scenes from an Accelerating Culture*, Crown Publishers, New York, 2000
Rise, Louisiana Museum of Modern Art, Humlebæk, 2002
Doug Aitken: A–Z Book (Fractals), The Fabric Workshop and Museum, Kunsthalle Zürich, Hatje Cantz, Ostfildern, 2003

CHANTAL AKERMAN
b. 1950, Brussels (Belgium); lives in Paris (France)

Select exhibitions
'Self-Portrait/Autobiography: a Work in Progress', Sean Kelly Gallery, New York; Frith Street Gallery, London, 1998
'Media City', Seoul Biennial, Seoul, 2000
Venice Biennale, Venice, 2001
Documenta 11, Kassel, 2002
'Micro Politics', Espai d'Art Contemporani de Castello, Castello, 2003

Select publications
Hall de Nuit, L'Arche Editeur, Paris, 1992
Un divan à New York, L'Arche Editeur, Paris, 1996
Une famille à Bruxelles, L'Arche Editeur, Paris, 1998

FRANCIS ALŸS
b. 1959, Antwerp (Belgium); lives in Mexico City (Mexico)

Select exhibitions
'Da Adversidade Vivemos', Musée d'Art Moderne de la Ville de Paris, Paris, 2001
'20 Million Mexicans Can't be Wrong', South London Gallery, London, 2002
'Cuando la fe mueve montañas – When Faith Moves Mountains', 3rd Bienal Iberoamericana de Lima, Lima, 2002
'Projects 76: Francis Alÿs – Modern Procession', Museum of Modern Art, New York, 2002
'Moving Pictures', Guggenheim, Bilbao, 2003
'Obra Pictórica', Museo Reina Sofia, Madrid; Kunsthaus Zürich, Zurich, 2003

Select publications
Francis Alÿs, Ivo Mequita and Bruce Ferguson, *Francis Alÿs: Walks/Paseos*, Museo de Arte Moderno, Mexico City, 1997
Cuauthémoc Medina, 'Francis Alÿs', *49 Biennale di Venezia*, Venice, 2001
Jörg Heiser, 'Walk on the Wild Side', *Frieze*, September 2002
Catherine Lampert, *Obra Pictórica*, Turner, Madrid, 2003
Francis Alÿs, *The Prophet and the Fly*, Turner, Madrid, 2003

LIZ ARNOLD
b. 1964, Perth (UK); d. 2001, London (UK)

Select exhibitions
Facts & Fictions Part 1, Galleria in Arco, Turin, 1998
Chicago Project Room, Chicago, 1999
Lotta Hammer, London, 1999
The Blood Show, Five Years, London, 1999
Galeria Mario Sequeira, Braga, 2000

Select publications
Chicken, Imprint 93, London, 1997
Facts & Fictions Part 1, Galleria in Arco, Turin, 1998
Liz Arnold, Lotta Hammer, London, 1999

JANET CARDIFF
b. 1957, Brussels, Ontario (Canada); lives in Berlin (Germany)

Select exhibitions
'The Paradise Institute', Canadian Pavilion, 49th Venice Biennale, Venice, 2001*
'Janet Cardiff and George Bures Miller: The Berlin Files', Portikus, Frankfurt, 2003
'Janet Cardiff and George Bures Miller: Recent Work', Whitechapel Art Gallery, London, 2003
'Black Hair', Central Park audio walk, Public Art Fund, New York, 2004
'The Berlin Files', Portikus, Frankfurt, 2004*
(*collaborations with George Bures Miller)

Select publications
Janet Cardiff, *The Missing Voice (case study b)*, Artangel, London, 1999
Elusive Paradise: The Millennium Prize, National Gallery of Canada, Ottawa, 2001
Carolyn Christov-Bakargiev, *Janet Cardiff: A Survey of Works including Collaborations with George Bures Miller*, P.S.1 Contemporary Art Center, New York, 2001
Nicole Armour, 'Suspending Disbelief: The Filmic Art of Janet Cardiff', *Cinemascope*, 2002
Aruna D'Souza, 'A World of Sound', *Art in America*, April 2002
Bennett Simpson, 'Walk On By', *Frieze*, April 2002
Janet Cardiff – George Bures Miller, Astrup Fearnley Museet for Moderne Kunst, Oslo, 2003

MAURIZIO CATTELAN
b. 1960, Padua (Italy); lives in New York (USA) and Milan (Italy)

Select exhibitions
'Project #65', Museum of Modern Art, New York, 1998
'Abracadabra', Tate Gallery, London, 1999
'Apocalypse: Beauty and Horror in Contemporary Art', Royal Academy of Arts, London, 2000
'Maurizio Cattelan', Färgfabriken, Stockholm, 2001
'Maurizio Cattelan', Marian Goodman Gallery, New York, 2002
'Public Affairs', Kunsthaus Zürich, Zurich, 2002
Deste Foundation for Contemporary Art, Athens, 2003
Museum Ludwig, Cologne, 2003
Museum of Contemporary Art, Los Angeles, 2003

Select publications
Permanent Food (edited with Paola Manfrin), nos 1–11, Les Presses du Réel, Dijon, 1989–2003
Maurizio Cattelan, 1995–1998, Le Consortium, Dijon; Centre d'Art Contemporain, Brétigny-sur-Orge; Galerie Emmanuel Perrotin, Paris, 1998
Maurizio Cattelan, 1997–1999, Edizioni Charta, Milan, 1999
6th Caribbean Biennial, Les Presses du Réel, Dijon, 2001
Francesco Bonami et al., *Maurizio Cattelan*, Phaidon, London, 2003

ADAM CHODZKO
b. 1965, London (UK); lives in Whitstable and London (UK)

Select exhibitions
'General Release', British Council selection for Venice Biennale, Scuola di San Pasquale, Venice, 1995
'It Always Jumps Back and Finds Its Own Way', Stichting De Appel, Amsterdam, 1997

'Sensation', Royal Academy of Arts, London, 1997
Ikon Gallery, Birmingham, 1999
'Artifice', Deste Foundation, Athens, 2000
'Micro/Macro: British Art 1996–2002', Mücsarnok
Kunsthalle, Budapest, 2003

Select publications
Jennifer Higgie et al., *Adam Chodzko*, August,
London, 1999
Chris Darke et al., *Plans and Spells: Adam
Chodzko*, Film and Video Umbrella, London, 2002
Adam Chodzko, *Romanov*, Book Works, London,
2002

NATHAN COLEY
b. 1967, Glasgow (UK); lives in Dundee (UK)

Select exhibitions
'The Land Marked', Centro Cultural de Belém,
Lisbon, 2001
'Happy Outsiders', Zacheta Panstwowa Galeria
Sztuki, Warsaw, 2002
'The Black Maria', The Physics Room (as part of
'Scape: Art & Industry Urban Biennial'),
Christchurch, 2002
'The Gap Show', Museum am Ostwall,
Dortmund, 2002
'Black Tent', Portsmouth Cathedral, Portsmouth,
2003
'Days Like These: The Tate Triennial of
Contemporary British Art', Tate Britain, London,
2003
'Independence', South London Gallery, London,
2003
'Showhome', North Shields, Newcastle, 2003

Select publications
Urban Sanctuary, Stills Gallery, Edinburgh, 1997
Nathan Coley – A Public Announcement, The
Changing Rooms, Stirling, 1999
Fourteen Churches of Münster, Westfälischer
Kunstverein, Münster, 2000
Black Tent, Art and Sacred Places, London, 2003
Days Like These, Tate Publishing, London, 2003

DOROTHY CROSS
b. 1956, Cork (Ireland); lives in Dublin (Ireland)

Select exhibitions
Venice Biennale, Venice, 1993
'Cry', ArtPace, San Antonio, Texas, 1996
'Even', Arnolfini, Bristol, 1997
5th International Istanbul Biennial, Istanbul, 1997
'Chiasm', Handball Alleys, St Enda's School,
Galway, Ireland, 1999
'Ghost Ship', Nissan Art Project, Dublin Bay,
1999
'Come into the Garden Maude', National Theatre,

London, commissioned by Public Art
Development Trust, 2002
'Liquid Sea', MOMA, Sydney, 2003

Select publications
Ebb, Douglas Hyde Gallery, Trinity College,
Dublin, 1988
Power House, ICA, Philadelphia, 1991
Even, Arnolfini, Bristol, 1997
Experiment: Conversations in Art and Science,
Wellcome Trust, London, 2003

JUAN CRUZ
b. 1970, Palencia (Spain); lives in London (UK)

Select exhibitions
'Driving Back', Camden Arts Centre, London, 2000
'Application for Planning Permit: Proposal to Build
a Metaphor', Melbourne Festival, Melbourne, 2001
'Portrait of a Sculptor', Matt's Gallery, London,
2001
'Squatters', Fundação de Serralves, Oporto; Witte
de With Center for Contemporary Art, Rotterdam,
2001
'Landing', Royal Holloway College, University of
London, London, 2002

Select publications
Ian Hunt and Simon Wallis, *Juan Cruz*, Kettle's
Yard, Cambridge, 1999
Juan Cruz, *Application for Planning Permit:
Proposal to Build a Metaphor*, Melbourne Festival,
Melbourne, 2001
Portrait of a Sculptor, Matt's Gallery, London, 2001
Bartomeu Mari, Juan Cruz, Tanja Elgeest, Angela
Ferreira and Filipa Oliveira, *Squatters*, Witte de
With Center for Contemporary Art, Rotterdam,
2001
*Landing: Eight Collaborative Projects Between
Artists and Geographers*, Royal Holloway College,
University of London, London, 2002

JEREMY DELLER
b. 1966, London (UK); lives in London

Select exhibitions
'Acid Brass', various locations, 1997 and ongoing
'Unconvention', Centre of Visual Arts, Cardiff, 1999
'Folk Archive', with Alan Kane, various locations,
1999 and ongoing
'Intelligence: New British Art 2000', Tate Britain,
London, 2000
'The Battle of Orgreave', commissioned by
Artangel, Orgreave, 2001
'Rock my World', Californian College of Arts and
Crafts, San Francisco, 2002
'Micro/Macro: British Art 1996–2002', Mücsarnok
Kunsthalle, Budapest, 2003

'Memory Bucket', ArtPace, San Antonio, Texas,
2003
'This Is Us', Center for Curatorial Studies, Bard
College, New York, 2003
'Turner Prize Exhibition', Tate Britain, London, 2004

Select publications
The Uses of Literacy, Book Works, London, 1999
The Battle of Orgreave, Artangel, London, 2001
Life is to Blame for Everything, Salon 3, London,
2001
After The Goldrush, CCAC Wattis Institute, San
Francisco, 2002
This Is Us, Center for Curatorial Studies, Bard
College, New York (CD and book), 2003

THOMAS DEMAND
b. 1964 in Munich (Germany); lives in Berlin
(Germany)

Select exhibitions
'New Photography', Museum of Modern Art, New
York, 1996
Kunsthalle Zürich, Zurich, 1998
Sydney Biennial, Sydney, 1998
'The Carnegie International', Carnegie Museum of
Art, Pittsburgh, 1999
Fondation Cartier, Paris, 2000
'Connivence', 6e Biennale de Lyon, Lyons, 2001
Lenbachhaus, Munich, 2002
Louisiana Museum of Modern Art, Humlebæk,
2003
Venice Biennale, Venice, 2003
São Paulo Biennale, São Paulo, 2004
Kunsthaus Bregenz, Bregenz, 2004

Select publications
Thomas Demand, Fondation Cartier, Paris;
Thames & Hudson, London, 2000
Thomas Demand, Aspen Art Museum, Aspen;
Stichting De Appel, Amsterdam, 2001
Thomas Demand (with Caruso St. John
Architects), Palazzo Pitti, Florence; Edizione
Pagliai Polistampa, Florence, 2001
Thomas Demand, Castello di Rivoli, Turin, 2002
Thomas Demand, Lenbachhaus, Munich;
Louisiana Museum of Modern Art, Humlebæk;
Schirmer/Mosel, Munich, 2002

ROD DICKINSON
b. 1965, Southampton (UK); lives in London (UK)

Select exhibitions
'From Hell', Cabinet Gallery, London, 1992
Cabinet Gallery, London, 1995
'Half-Lit World', Camerawork, London, 1998
'Off the Grid', Lehman Maupin Gallery, New York,
2002

'All You Need To Know', Laing Art Gallery, Newcastle, 2002

'Independence', South London Gallery, London, 2003

'The Tenth Level', Centre for Contemporary Art, Glasgow, 2004

Select publications

Sarah Kent, *Shark Infested Waters: The Saatchi Collection of British Art in the 90s*, Zwemmer, London, 1994

The Saatchi Decade: Young British Art, Booth-Clibborn, London, 1999

Adam Parfrey (ed.), *Apocalypse Culture II: The Jonestown Reenactment*, Feral House, Los Angeles, 2000

Hurts So Good, CAC, Vilnius, Lithuania, 2003

Steve Rushton (ed.), *The Milgram Re-enactment*, Jan van Eyck Academie, Maastricht, 2003

WILLIE DOHERTY
b. 1959, Derry (UK); lives in Derry

Select exhibitions

'The British Art Show', McLellan Galleries, Glasgow, City Art Gallery, Leeds; Hayward Gallery, London, 1990

'Unknown Depths', ICA, London; John Hansard Gallery, Southampton; Angel Row Gallery, Nottingham, 1991

'An Irish Presence', Venice Biennale, Venice, 1993

'Turner Prize Exhibition', Tate Gallery, London, 1994

'In The Dark, Projected Works', Kunsthalle Bern, Berne, 1996

'Somewhere Else', Tate Gallery, Liverpool, 1998

'The Carnegie International', Carnegie Museum of Art, Pittsburgh, 1999

'True Nature', Renaissance Society, Chicago, 1999

'False Memory', Irish Museum of Modern Art, Dublin, 2002

Select publications

Ian Hunt and Camilla Jackson, *Willie Doherty: Somewhere Else*, Tate Gallery, Liverpool, 1998

Daniel Jewesbury, *How It Was*, Ormeau Baths Gallery, Belfast, 2001

Carolyn Christov-Bakargiev and Caoimhín Mac Giolla Leith, *False Memory*, Irish Museum of Modern Art, Dublin; Merrill, London, 2002

A. K. DOLVEN
b. 1953, Oslo, Norway; lives in London

Select exhibitions

6th International Istanbul Biennial, Istanbul, 1999

'Century of Innocence', Rooseum Center for Contemporary Art, Malmö, 2000

'The Other Side of Zero', Tate Gallery, Liverpool, 2000

Kunsthalle Bern, Berne, 2001

'On the Way to the Screen: Video of the 90s', Central House of Artists, Moscow, 2001

'Headlights', Henie Onstad Kunstsenter, Oslo, 2002

'Malerei ohne Malerei', Museum der Bildenden Künste, Leipzig, 2002

'Artist of the Year', Bergen Art Hall, Bergen, 2004

Select publications

januar, published by A. K. Dolven, London, 1998

Anne Katrine Dolven, Kunsthalle Bern, Berne, 2001

it could happen to you, Film and Video Umbrella, London, 2002

2002, Staatliches Museum Schwerin, Schwerin, 2002

STAN DOUGLAS
b. 1960, Vancouver (Canada); lives in Vancouver

Select exhibitions

'Stan Douglas', Salzburger Kunstverein, Salzburg, 1998

'Double Vision: Stan Douglas and Douglas Gordon', Dia Center for the Arts, New York, 1999

'Stan Douglas', Vancouver Art Gallery, Vancouver, travelling exhibition, 1999

'Between Cinema and a Hard Place', Tate Modern, London, 2000

'Stan Douglas: Le Détroit', Kunsthalle Basel, Basel, 2001

Venice Biennale, Venice, 2001

Documenta 11, Kassel, 2002

São Paulo Biennale, São Paulo, 2002

'Stan Douglas', Serpentine Gallery, London, 2002

'Stan Douglas: Film Installations and Photographs', Kestner Gesellschaft, Hanover, 2003

Select publications

Double Vision: Stan Douglas and Douglas Gordon, Dia Center for the Arts, New York, 2000

Stan Douglas, Kunsthalle Basel, Basel, 2001

Documenta 11_ Platform 5: Exhibition, Hatje Cantz, Ostfildern, 2002

Journey into Fear, Serpentine Gallery, London, 2002

Stan Douglas: Film Installationen, Kestner Gesellschaft, Hanover, 2003

LEIF ELGGREN
b. 1950, Linköping (Sweden); lives in Stockholm (Sweden)

Select exhibitions

'Dream Machines', Hayward Gallery, London, 2000

'Flown Over By An Old King', Färgfabriken, Stockholm, 2000

'The North is Protected', Nordic Pavilion, Venice Biennale, Venice, 2001

'As if I was my Father', Galleri Thomas Ehrngren, Stockholm, 2002

'New Jerusalem' (with C. M. von Hausswolff), Pierogi Gallery, New York, 2002

'Todos Somos Pecadores', Museo Rufino Tamayo, Mexico City, 2002

'Transformer', Pori Art Museum, Pori, 2002

'Utopia Station', Venice Biennale, Venice, 2003

Select publications

Royal Restlessness, Firework Edition, Stockholm, 1993

Experiment with Dreams, Firework Edition, Stockholm, 1996

Yellow & Black, Firework Edition, Stockholm, 1997

Names, Firework Edition, Stockholm, 1998

Flown Over By An Old King, Färgfabriken, Stockholm, 2000

OLAFUR ELIASSON
b. 1967, Copenhagen (Denmark); lives in Berlin (Germany)

Select exhibitions

São Paulo Biennial, São Paulo, 1998

'The Carnegie International', Carnegie Museum of Art, Pittsburgh, 1999

'Wonderland', St Louis Museum of Art, St Louis, 2000

'Surroundings Surrounded', ZKM, Karlsruhe, 2001

'The Mediated Motion', Kunsthaus Bregenz, Bregenz, 2001

'Chaque matin, je me sens différent – chaque soir je me sens le même', Musée d'Art Moderne de la Ville de Paris, Paris, 2002

'el aire es azul – the air is blue', Luis Barragán House, Mexico City, 2002

'The Blind Pavilion', Venice Biennale, Venice, 2003

'The Weather Project', Turbine Hall, Tate Modern, London, 2003

Select publications

Olafur Eliasson: The Curious Garden, Kunsthalle Basel, Basel, 1997

Peter Weibel (ed.), *Olafur Eliasson: Surroundings Surrounded*, Neue Galerie am Landesmuseum Joanneum, Graz; ZKM, Karlsruhe; MIT Press, Cambridge, Mass. and London, 2001

Daniel Birnbaum et al., *Olafur Eliasson*, Phaidon, London, 2003

Olafur Eliasson et al., *Olafur Eliasson: The Blind Pavilion*, Hatje Cantz, Ostfildern, 2003

Susan May (ed.), *Olafur Eliasson: The Weather Project*, Tate Modern, London, 2003

FISCHLI/WEISS
Peter Fischli: b. 1952, Zurich (Switzerland); lives in Zürich
David Weiss: b. 1946, Zurich (Switzerland); lives in Zürich

Select exhibitions
Swiss Pavilion, Venice Biennale, Venice, 1995
'Voilà: le monde dans la tête', Musée d'Art Moderne de la Ville de Paris, Paris, 2000
'Sichtbare Welt, Plötzlich diese Übersicht, Grosse Fragen-Kleine Fragen', Museum für Gegenwartskunst, Basel, 2000
'Fragen Projektion', Museum Ludwig, Cologne, 2002
'Wallflowers: Grosse Fotografien', Kunsthaus Zürich, Zurich, 2002
'Grotesk! 130 Jahre der Frechheit', Haus der Kunst, Munich, 2003
Museum Boijmans Van Beuningen, Rotterdam, 2003
'Utopia Station', Venice Biennale, Venice, 2003

Select publications
Peter Fischli/David Weiss, *Airports*, Scalo, Zurich, 1990
Peter Fischli/David Weiss, *Bilder Ansichten*, Scalo, Zurich, 1991
Peter Fischli/David Weiss, Musée d'Art Moderne de la Ville de Paris, Paris; Verlag der Buchhandlung Walther König, Cologne, 1999
Peter Fischli/David Weiss, *Sichtbare Welt*, Verlag der Buchhandlung Walther König, Cologne, 2000
Marjorie Jongbloed and Kaspar König (eds), *Peter Fischli/David Weiss Fragen Projektion*, Museum Ludwig, Cologne, 2002

LIAM GILLICK
b. 1964, Aylesbury (UK); lives in London (UK) and New York (USA)

Select exhibitions
Documenta 10, Kassel, 1997
'What If', Moderna Museet, Stockholm, 2000
'The Wood Way', Whitechapel Gallery, London, 2002
'Adorno 100', Frankfurter Kunstverein, Frankfurt, 2003
'Communes, Bar and Greenrooms', Power Plant Contemporary Art Gallery, Toronto, 2003
'Literally', Museum of Modern Art, New York, 2003
'Telling Histories', Kunstverein München, Munich, 2003
'Turner Prize Exhibition', Tate Britain, London, 2003
Venice Biennale, Venice, 2003

Select publications
Erasmus is Late, Book Works, London, 1995
Discussion Island/Big Conference Centre,
Kunstverein Ludwigsburg, Ludwigsburg; Orchard Gallery, Derry, 1997
Liam Gillick, Oktagon, Cologne; Lukas & Sternberg, New York, 2000
Five or Six, Lukas & Sternberg, New York, 2001
Literally No Place, Book Works, London, 2002

DOMINIQUE GONZALEZ-FOERSTER
b. 1965, Strasbourg (France); lives in Paris (France)

Select exhibitions
'Traffic', CAPC Musée d'Art Contemporain, Bordeaux, 1996
'Cities on the Move', Secession, Vienna; CAPC Musée d'Art Contemporain, Bordeaux, 1997
'88:88', Kaiser Wilhelm Museum, Krefeld, 1998
'Gonzalez-Foerster, Huyghe, Parreno', ARC-Musée d'Art Moderne de la Ville de Paris, Paris, 1998
'Manifesta 2', Luxembourg, 1998
'Tropicale Modernité', Pavello Mies van der Rohe, Barcelona, 1999
'Dominique Gonzalez-Foerster, Philippe Parreno, Pierre Huyghe', Kunstverein Hamburg, Hamburg, 2000
'Exotourisme', Centre Georges Pompidou, Paris, 2002
Documenta 11, Kassel, 2002
'Staging Space, Suggesting a Story', Museum Boijmans Van Beuningen, Rotterdam, 2003
'Utopia Station', Venice Biennale, Venice, 2003

Select publications
Dominique Gonzalez-Foerster, Pierre Huyghe, Philippe Parreno, Musée d'Art Moderne de la Ville de Paris, Paris, 1998
Dominique Gonzalez-Foerster and Jens Hoffmann (ed.), *Tropicale Modernité*, Fundació Mies van der Rohe, Barcelona, 1999
Stéphanie Moisdon-Trembley, *Dominique Gonzalez-Foerster*, Hazan, Paris, 2002
Dominique Gonzalez-Foerster, *Films*, Portikus, Frankfurt; Le Consortium, Dijon, 2003

DAN GRAHAM
b. 1942, Urbana, Illinois (USA); lives in New York (USA)

Select exhibitions
Documenta 5, Kassel, 1972
'Ambiente Arte', Venice Biennial, Venice, 1976
Museum of Modern Art, Oxford, 1978
Museum of Modern Art, New York, 1980
'Westkunst', Museen der Stadt Köln, Cologne, 1981
'Dan Graham: The Suburban City', Museum für Gegenwartskunst, Basel, 1996
'Dan Graham', Centro Galego de Arte
Contemporánea, Santiago de Compostela, 1997
Documenta 10, Kassel, 1997
'Into the Light', Whitney Museum of American Art, New York, 2001
'Dan Graham Works 1965–2000', Fundação de Serralves, Oporto; ARC-Musée d'Art Moderne de la Ville de Paris, Paris; Kröller-Müller Museum, Otterlo; Kunsthalle Düsseldorf, Düsseldorf, 2002–3

Select publications
Dan Graham, *For Publication*, Otis Art Institute, Los Angeles, 1975.
Dan Graham: Rock My Religion. Writings and Art Projects 1965–1990, ed. Brian Wallis, MIT Press, Cambridge, Mass., 1993
Two Way Mirror Power, MIT Press, Cambridge, Mass., 1999
Marianne Brouwer et al., *Dan Graham: Works 1965–2000*, Richter Verlag, Düsseldorf, 2001
Beatriz Colomina et al., *Dan Graham*, Phaidon, London, 2001

RODNEY GRAHAM
b. 1949, Vancouver (Canada); lives in Vancouver

Select exhibitions
'Rodney Graham', Art Gallery of York University, Toronto, Ontario; Yves Gevaert, Brussels; Renaissance Society, Chicago, Illinois, 1994–96
Canadian Pavilion, Venice Biennale, Venice, 1997
'Rodney Graham: Cinema, Music, Video', Kunsthalle Wien, Vienna, 1999
'…the nearest faraway place…', with Bruce Nauman, Dia Center for the Arts, New York, 2000
'Rodney Graham', Whitechapel Art Gallery, London; Kunstsammlung, Nordrhein-Westfalen, Düsseldorf; MAC Galeries Contemporaines des Musées de Marseille, Marseilles, 2002
'Rodney Graham: A Little Thought', Art Gallery of Ontario, Toronto; Museum of Contemporary Art, Los Angeles; Vancouver Art Gallery, Vancouver, 2004–5

Select publications
Rodney Graham: Cinema Music Video, Kunsthalle Wien, Vienna; Yves Gevaert Verlag, Brussels (with audio CD), 1999
Rodney Graham, *Getting it Together in the Country, Some Works with Sound Waves, Some Works with Light Waves and Some Other Experimental Works*, Kunstverein München, Munich; Westfälischer Kunstverein, Münster (with vinyl record), 2000
Rodney Graham, Whitechapel Art Gallery, London, 2002
Rodney Graham: A Little Thought, Art Gallery of Ontario, Toronto; Museum of Contemporary Art, Los Angeles; Vancouver Art Gallery, Vancouver, 2004

GRAHAM GUSSIN
b. 1960, London (UK); lives in London

Select exhibitions
'British Art Show', Edinburgh, Southampton,
Cardiff, Birmingham, 2000
'Graham Gussin', Galerie Chantal Crousel, Paris,
2001
'Nothing', Northern Gallery for Contemporary Art,
Sunderland; Rooseum Center for Contemporary
Art, Malmö, 2001
'States of Mind', New Museum of Contemporary
Art, New Media Space, New York; Goldie Paley
Gallery/Moore College of Art and Design,
Philadelphia, 2001
'En Route', Serpentine Gallery, London, 2002
'Graham Gussin', Ikon Gallery, Birmingham, 2002
'Something Else', Primo Piano, Rome, 2002
'Graham Gussin', Lisson Gallery, London, 2003
'Stopover', Venice Biennale, Henry Moore
Foundation Contemporary Projects, 2003
'The Distance Between Me and You', Lisson
Gallery, London, 2003

Select publications
Graham Gussin, Ikon Gallery, Birmingham, 2002
Intelligence: New British Art 2000, Tate
Publishing, London, 2000
Graham Gussin and Ele Carpenter (eds),
Nothing, August, London; Northern Gallery for
Contemporary Art, Sunderland, 2001
Graham Gussin, Remote Viewer, Film and Video
Umbrella, London, 2002

IAN HAMILTON FINLAY
b. 1925, Nassau (Bahamas); lives in Stonypath
(UK)

Select exhibitions
'Instruments of the Revolution and Other Works',
ICA, London, 1992
'Works: Pure and Political', Deichtorhallen,
Hamburg, 1995
'Variation on Several Themes', Joan Miró
Foundation, Barcelona, 1999
'Nature Over Again After Poussin', McMaster
Museum of Art, Hamilton, Ontario, 2000
'Maritime Works', Tate St Ives, 2002

Select publications
Yves Abrioux (ed.), Ian Hamilton Finlay: A Visual
Primer, Reaktion Books, London, 1994
Zdenek Felix and Pia Simig (eds), Ian Hamilton
Finlay: Works in Europe 1974–1995, Hatje
Cantz, Ostfildern, 1995
Robin Gillanders, Little Sparta, National Galleries
of Scotland, Edinburgh, 1998
Ian Hamilton Finlay: Maritime Works, Tate
Publishing, St Ives, 2002

CARL MICHAEL VON HAUSSWOLFF
b. 1956, Linköping (Sweden); lives in Stockholm
(Sweden)

Select exhibitions
CCA, Kitakyushu, 2001
'The North is Protected', Nordic Pavilion, Venice
Biennale, Venice, 2001
'Todos Somos Pecadores', Museo Rufino Tamayo,
Mexico City, 2002
'New Jerusalem' (with Leif Elggren), Pierogi
Gallery, New York, 2002
Galerija Miroslav Kraljevic, Zagreb, 2003
Nicola Fornello, Prato, 2003
'Utopia Station' (with Leif Elggren), Venice
Biennale, Venice, 2003

Select publications
The North Is Protected, Nordic Pavilion; Sähkö,
Helsinki, 2001
Sound Art: The Swedish Scene, Svensk Musik,
Stockholm, 2001
142 Reasons for Still Being Alive, CCA,
Kitakyushu, 2002
Stun Shelter, Nicola Fornello/Allquestions, Prato,
2003
Thomas More's Utopia Incorporated by KREV,
Venice Biennale; Firework Edition, Stockholm,
2003

SUSAN HILLER
b. 1942, Tallahassee, Florida (USA); lives in Berlin
(Germany)

Select exhibitions
'Susan Hiller', Gallery House, London, 1973
'Susan Hiller', ICA, London, 1986
'Now/Here', Louisiana Museum of Modern Art,
Humlebæk, 1996
'Susan Hiller', Tate Gallery, Liverpool, 1996
'Out of Actions', Museum of Contemporary Art,
Los Angeles, 1998
'The Muse in the Museum', Museum of Modern
Art, New York, 1999
Bienal de la Habana, Havana, 2000
'Witness', Artangel, London, 2000
Sydney Biennale, Sydney, 2002
'Susan Hiller', BALTIC, Gateshead, 2004

Select publications
Jean Fisher, Susan Hiller: The Revenants of Time,
Matt's Gallery, London, 1990
Susan Hiller, After the Freud Museum, Book
Works, London, 1995
Barbara Einzig (ed.), Thinking About Art:
Conversations with Susan Hiller, Manchester
University Press, Manchester, 1996
Guy Brett, Rebecca Cochran and Stuart Morgan,
Susan Hiller, Tate Gallery, Liverpool, 1996

Louise Milne, Marianne Bech and Mette Marcus,
Susan Hiller, Museet for Samtidskunst, Roskilde,
2002

RONI HORN
b. 1955, New York (US); lives in New York

Select exhibitions
'You are the Weather', Museum für
Gegenwartskunst, Basel, 1998
'Events of Relation', Musée d'Art Moderne de la
Ville de Paris, Paris, 1999
'Still Water (The River Thames, for Example)',
Whitney Museum of American Art, New York, 2000
'Blah, blah, blah, your hair, Blah, blah, blah,
your eyes; Blah, blah, blah, blah, care, Blah,
blah, blah, blah, skies', Dia Center for the Arts,
New York, 2001
'The Citibank Private Bank Photography Prize
2001: Roni Horn, Hellen van Meene, Boris
Mikhailov, Jem Southam, and Hannah Starkey',
The Photographers' Gallery, London, 2001
'Moving Pictures', Solomon R. Guggenheim
Museum, New York, 2002
'Tempo', Museum of Modern Art, New York, 2002
'Roni Horn: Dessins/Drawings', Centre Georges
Pompidou, Paris, 2003
'If on a Winter's Night…Roni Horn…',
Fotomuseum Winterthur, Winterthur, 2003
'Stretch', Power Plant Contemporary Art Gallery,
Toronto, 2003

Select publications
Roni Horn, TO PLACE: (v1) Bluff Life, 1990,
(v2) Folds, 1991, (v3) Lava, 1992, (v4) Pooling
Water, 1994, (v5) Verne's Journey, 1995, (v6)
Haraldsdóttir, 1996, (v7) Arctic Circles, 1998,
(v8) Becoming a Landscape, 2001, various
publishers, United States and Germany (ongoing)
Roni Horn, Another Water (The River Thames, for
Example), Scalo, Zurich and New York, 2000
Lynne Cooke et al., Roni Horn, Phaidon, London,
2000
Thierry de Duve, Paulo Herkenhoff et al., If on a
Winter's Night…Roni Horn…, Fotomuseum
Winterthur, Winterthur; Steidl, Göttingen, 2003
Roni Horn, Cabinet of, Steidl/Dangin, Göttingen
and New York, 2003

DOUGLAS HUEBLER
b. 1924, Ann Arbor, Michigan (USA); d. 1997

Select exhibitions
Van Abbemuseum, Eindhoven, 1979
FRAC, Limousin, 1993
'Voilà: le monde dans la tête', Musee d'Art
Moderne de la Ville de Paris, Paris, 2000
Camden Arts Centre, London, 2002

Select publications
Location Piece # 2: New York City – Seattle, Washington, Multiples Inc., New York, 1970
Durata Duration, Sperone Gallery, Turin, 1970
Variable Piece 4, Secrets, Printed Matter Inc., New York, 1973
Crocodile Tears, Visual Studies Workshop Press, Rochester, NY, 1985

STEPHEN HUGHES
b. 1968, Brighton (UK); lives in Brighton

Select exhibitions
De La Warr Pavilion, Bexhill-on-Sea, 2001
Galerie du Pole Image, Rouen, 2002
Photofusion, London, 2002
'Art Cologne', Cologne, 2003
'Art Frankfurt', Frankfurt, 2003
Blue Sky Gallery, Portland, Oregon 2003
'Paris Photo', Paris, 2003

Select publications
Insight Magazine, Photoworks, January 2000
Camera Austria, no. 75, 2001
Portfolio: the Catalogue of Contemporary Photography in Britain, no. 34, 2001
Stephen Hughes Photographs, De La Warr Pavilion, Bexhill-on-Sea; Photoworks, Maidstone, 2001
Tema Celeste, no. 88/89, January–February 2002
art: das Kunst magazin, November 2003

MARINE HUGONNIER
b. 1969, Paris (France); lives in London (UK)

Select exhibitions
Centro Galego de Arte Contemporánea, Santiago de Compostela, 2001
'Impact', Yokohama Red Brick Warehouse Number 1, Yokohama, 2003
'Utopia Station', Venice Biennale, Venice, 2003
Dundee Contemporary Arts, Dundee, 2004

Select publications
Interlude, Galerie Chantal Crousel, Paris, 2000
Marine Hugonnier, Centro Galego de Arte Contemporánea, Santiago de Compostela, 2001
Marine Hugonnier, Dundee Contemporary Arts, Dundee; Film and Video Umbrella, London, 2004

PIERRE HUYGHE
b. 1962, Paris (France); lives in Paris and New York (USA)

Select exhibitions
'The Carnegie International', Carnegie Museum of Art, Pittsburgh, 1999

'The Third Memory', Centre Georges Pompidou, Paris, 2000
French Pavilion, Venice Biennale, Venice, 2001
Documenta 11, Kassel, Germany, 2002
'L'expédition scintillante: A musical', Kunsthaus Bregenz, Bregenz, 2002
'Moving Pictures', Guggenheim Museum, New York, 2002
'No Ghost Just a Shell', Institute for Visual Culture, Cambridge; San Francisco Museum of Modern Art, San Francisco, 2002
'Streamside Day Follies', Dia Center of the Arts, New York, 2003
'The Hugo Boss Prize 2002 Exhibition', Guggenheim Museum, New York, 2003

Select publications
Pierre Huyghe, Kunstverein München, Munich; Kunsthalle Zürich, Zurich; Secession, Vienna; Le Consortium, Dijon, 2000
The Third Memory, Centre Georges Pompidou, Paris; Renaissance Society, Chicago, 2000
Pierre Huyghe, *Le Château de Turing*, Le Consortium, Dijon; Van Abbemuseum, Eindhoven, 2003
Pierre Huyghe and Philippe Parreno, *No Ghost Just A Shell*, Verlag der Buchhandlung Walther König, Cologne, 2003

BODYS ISEK KINGELEZ
b. 1948, Kimbembele Ihunga (Democratic Republic of the Congo); lives in Kinshasa (Democratic Republic of the Congo)

Select exhibitions
'Bodys Isek Kingelez', Fondation Cartier pour l'Art Contemporain, Paris, 1995
'Bodys Isek Kingelez', Kunstverein Hamburg, Hamburg, 2000–1
'The Short Century', P.S.1, New York; Museum of Contemporary Art, Chicago; House of World Cultures, Martin-Gropius-Bau, Berlin; Museum Villa Stuck, Munich, 2001–2
'Bodys Isek Kingelez', Villa Stuck, Munich, 2002
Documenta 11, Kassel, 2002
'Bodys Isek Kingelez', Centre Culturel Wolu-Culture, La Médiatine, Brussels, 2003
'The American Effect: Global Perspectives on the United States, 1990–2003', Whitney Museum of American Art, New York, 2003

Select publications
Bodys Isek Kingelez, Fondation Cartier, Paris, 1995
Okwui Enwezor et al., *Bodys Isek Kingelez*, Kunstverein Hamburg, Hamburg; Hatje Cantz, Ostfildern, 2001
Okwui Enwezor et al., *The Short Century, Independence and Liberation Movements in*

Africa, 1945–1994, Prestel, Munich, 2001
The American Effect: Global Perspectives on the United States, 1990–2003, Whitney Museum of American Art, New York, 2003

JOACHIM KOESTER
b. 1962, Copenhagen (Denmark); lives in New York (USA)

Select exhibitions
Johannesburg Biennale, Johannesburg, 1997
Documenta 10, Kassel, 1997
'Nuit Blanche', Musée d'Art Moderne de la Ville de Paris, Paris, 1998
Arnolfini, Bristol, 2000
Greene Naftali Gallery, New York, 2000
Centre National de la Photographie, Paris, 2001
Statens Museum for Kunst, Copenhagen, 2001
Kunsthalle Nürnberg, Nuremberg, 2002

Select publications
Joachim Koester, *Day for Night, Christiania 1996*, Gallerie Nicolai Wallner, Copenhagen, 1998
Art at the Turn of the Millennium, Taschen, Cologne, 1999
Sandra of the Tuliphouse (with Matthew Buckingham), Statens Museum for Kunst, Copenhagen, 2001
Joachim Koester, *Row Housing*, Galleri Nicolai Wallner, Copenhagen, 2002
Joachim Koester, *different stories, different places*, Kunsthalle Nürnberg, Nuremberg, 2002

KOMAR & MELAMID
Vitaly Komar: b. 1943, Moscow (Russia); lives in New York (USA)
Alex Melamid: b. 1945, Moscow (Russia); lives in New York (USA)

Select exhibitions
'Grand Lobby Installation', Brooklyn Museum, New York, 1990
'Komar & Melamid, Die Beliebten und Ungeliebten Bilder', Museum Ludwig, Cologne, 1997
'Symbols of the Big Bang', Yeshiva University Museum, Center for Jewish History, New York, 2002–3

Select publications
Carter Ratcliff, *Komar & Melamid*, Abbeville Press, New York, 1988
JoAnn Wypijewski, ed., *Painting by Numbers: Komar and Melamid's Scientific Guide to Art*, Farrar Straus and Giroux, New York, 1997
Mia Fineman, *When Elephants Paint: The Quest of Two Russian Artists to Save the Elephants of Thailand: Komar & Melamid*, Harper Collins, New York, 2000

SHARON LOCKHART
b. 1964, Norwood, Mass. (USA); lives in Los Angeles (USA)

Select exhibitions
Künstlerhaus Stuttgart, Stuttgart, 1995
'Cinéma Cinéma, Contemporary Art and the Cinematic Experience', Van Abbemuseum, Eindhoven, 1999
neugerriemschneider, Berlin, 1999
'Elysian Fields', Centre Georges Pompidou, Paris, 2000
'Whitney Biennial', Whitney Museum of American Art, New York, 2000
'Teatro Amazonas', Museum Boijmans Van Beuningen, Rotterdam; Kunsthalle Zürich, Zurich; Kunstmuseum Wolfsburg, Wolfsburg, 2000
6e Biennale de Lyon, Lyons, 2001
'Abbild', Landesmuseum Joanneum, Graz, 2001
'Interview Locations/Family Photographs', Blum & Poe, Santa Monica, 2001
Museum of Contemporary Art, Chicago, 2001
'Public Offerings', Museum of Contemporary Art, Los Angeles, 2001
Barbara Gladstone Gallery, New York, 2003
'Fast Forward. Media Art', Sammlung Goetz, ZKM, Karlsruhe, 2003

Select publications
Sharon Lockhart: Teatro Amazonas, Museum Boijmans Van Beuningen, Rotterdam, 2000
Sharon Lockhart, Museum of Contemporary Art, Chicago; Hatje Cantz, Ostfildern, 2001

KATRIN VON MALTZAHN
b. 1964, Rostock (Germany); lives in Berlin (Germany)

Select exhibitions
'Trial & Failure', Taidehalli, Helsinki, 1997
'Wort-Welten/Schrift-Bilder', Berlinische Galerie, Berlin, 1998
'Einigkeit, Recht und Freiheit', Martin Gropius Bau, Berlin, 1999
'Window Views', Galerie Barbara Wien, Berlin, 1999
'Biennale Balticum', Rauma, 2000
'iHop', Lunds Konsthall, Lund, 2000
'my private languages 1', Kunstraum München, Munich, 2000
'Archives alive', BüroFriedrich, Berlin, 2002
'Svenska för invandrare', gallery BOX, Gothenburg, 2002
'my private languages 2', Akershus Kunstnersenter, Lillestrøm, 2003

Select publications
Katrin von Maltzahn 1994–96, Künstlerhaus Bethanien, Berlin, 1996

Katrin von Maltzahn 1996–99, Wiens Verlag, Berlin, 1999
Katrin von Maltzahn: Living Archive, BüroFriedrich, Berlin, 2002

ALEXANDER AND SUSAN MARIS
Alexander Maris b. 1960, Scotland; Susan Maris b. 1966, Norfolk (UK); both live in Blantyre (UK)

Select exhibitions
'Momenta', Lisson Gallery, London, 1996
'Matter', Stills, Edinburgh, 1999
'Therapeuticum', RAM Galleri, Oslo, 1999
'escape', Media_City Seoul, Seoul, 2000
'Re:mote', The Photographers' Gallery, London, 2002

Select publications
Graham Gussin and Ele Carpenter (eds), Nothing, August, London; Northern Gallery for Contemporary Art, Sunderland, 2001
Ross Birrell and Alec Finlay (eds), Justified Sinners, Pocketbooks, Edinburgh, 2002
Friday 8 May, Morning Star, Newcastle; BALTIC, Gateshead, 2003

STEVE MCQUEEN
b. 1969, London (UK); lives in Amsterdam (Netherlands)

Select exhibitions
'Spellbound', Hayward Gallery, London, 1996
'Deadpan', Museum of Modern Art, Project Room, New York, 1997
Museum Boijmans Van Beuningen, Rotterdam, 1998
'Steve McQueen', Institute of Contemporary Art, London, 1999
'Turner Prize Exhibition', Tate Gallery, London, 1999
'Mirror's Edge', Vancouver Art Gallery, Vancouver, British Columbia, 2001
'Public Offerings', Museum of Contemporary Art, Los Angeles, 2001
'Caribs' Leap/Western Deep', Artangel at Lumière, London, 2002
Documenta 11, Kassel, 2002
ARC-Musée d'Art Moderne de la Ville de Paris, Paris, 2003
'Tate Egg Live', Tate Britain, London, 2003 (one-time performance)

Select publications
Steve McQueen, Stedelijk Van Abbemuseum, Eindhoven, 1997
Steve McQueen, Institute of Contemporary Art, London; Kunsthalle Zürich, Zurich, 1999
Steve McQueen, Kunsthalle Wien, Vienna, 2001
Jean Fisher, Steve McQueen, Caribs' Leap/

Western Deep, Artangel, London; Documenta 11, Kassel; Fundação de Serralves, Oporto; Fundació Antoni Tàpies, Barcelona, 2002
Hans Ulrich Obrist et al., Steve McQueen, Speaking in Tongues, Musée d'Art Moderne de la Ville de Paris, Paris, 2003

BORIS MIKHAILOV
b. 1938, Kharkov (Ukraine); lives in Kharkov and Berlin (Germany)

Select exhibitions
'Boris Mikhailov', Portikus, Frankfurt, 1995
'Boris Mikhailov', Kunsthalle Zürich, Zurich, 1996
'Boris Mikhailov', Stedelijk Museum, Amsterdam, 1998
'Les Misérables (About the World)', Sprengel Museum, Hanover, 1998
'Boris Mikhailov', Centre National de la Photographie, Paris, 1999
'Boris Mikhailov', The Photographers' Gallery, London, 2000
'How you look at it', Sprengel Museum, Hanover; Städelsches Kunstinstitut, Frankfurt, 2000
'2000 Hasselblad Award Winner', Hasselblad Center, Gothenburg, Sweden, 2000
'Case History', Saatchi Gallery, London, 2001
'From the 60s until now…', Museum of Modern Art, New York, 2001
'Case History', Frans Hals Museum, Haarlem, 2003
'Cruel + Tender: The Real in the Twentieth-Century Photograph', Tate Modern, London; Museum Ludwig, Cologne, 2003
'Retrospective', Fotomuseum Winterthur, Winterthur, 2003

Select publications
Boris Mikhailov, Stedelijk Museum, Amsterdam, 1998
Boris Mikhailov: Case History, Scalo, Zurich, 1999
Gunilla Knape (ed.), Boris Mikhailov: The Hasselblad Award 2000, Hasselblad Center, Gothenburg, 2000
Gilda Williams, 55 Boris Mikhailov, Phaidon, London, 2001
Boris Mikhailov: A Retrospective, Fotomuseum Winterthur, Winterthur; Scalo, Zurich, 2003

GUY MORETON
b. 1971, Lincoln (UK); lives in Southampton (UK)

Select exhibitions
'It's Your Turn', Kettle's Yard, Cambridge, 2001
'Wegrecht' (with Alec Finlay), Torhaus Rombergpark, Dortmund, 2002
'Generator', Spacex Gallery, Exeter; Liverpool Biennial; The Minories, Colchester, 2002–3

'Right of Way' (with Alec Finlay), Galway Arts Centre, Galway, 2004

Select publications
Football Haiku, (ed. Alec Finlay), Pocketbooks Edinburgh; BALTIC, Gateshead, 2002
Irish 2 (with Alec Finlay), BALTIC, Gateshead; Spacex, Exeter; Morning Star, Newcastle, 2002
There Where You Are Not – Wittgenstein's Wandering (with Alec Finlay and Dr Michael Nedo), Black Dog Publishing, London and New York, 2005

JUN NGUYEN-HATSUSHIBA
b. 1968, Tokyo (Japan); lives in Ho Chi Minh City (Vietnam)

Select exhibitions
'Memorial Project Minamata: Neither Either Nor Neither – A Love Story', Mizuma Art Gallery, Tokyo, 2002
'Jun Nguyen-Hatsushiba/MATRIX 203: Memorial Project Vietnam', UC Berkeley Art Museum, Berkeley; New Museum of Contemporary Art, New York, 2003
MACRO, Museo d'Arte Contemporanea Roma, Rome, 2003
'Memorial Project Nha Trang, Vietnam: Towards the Complex – For the Courageous, the Curious, and the Cowards', MIT List Visual Arts Center, Cambridge, Mass., 2003
'Poetic Justice', 8th International Istanbul Biennial, Istanbul, 2003
'The Moderns', Castello di Rivoli Museo d'Arte Contemporanea, Turin, 2003
'Z.O.U – Zone of Urgency', Venice Biennale, Venice, 2003

Select publications
Haruko Tomisawa, *Attitude 2002 – One Truth in Your Heart*, Contemporary Art Museum, Kumamoto, 2002
Yuko Hasegawa et al., *Jun Nguyen-Hatsushiba*, MACRO, Museo d'Arte Contemporanea Roma, Rome, 2003
Carolyn Christov-Bakargiev (ed.), *The Moderns*, Castello di Rivoli Museo d'Arte Contemporanea, Turin, 2003
Heidi Zuckerman Jacobson, *MATRIX 203/Jun Nguyen-Hatsushiba: Memorial Project Vietnam*, UC Berkeley Art Museum, Berkeley, 2003

PAUL NOBLE
b. 1963, Northumberland (UK); lives in London (UK)

Select exhibitions
'NOBSON', Chisenhale Gallery, London, 1998

'Protest & Survive', Whitechapel Art Gallery, London, 2000
Interim Art, London, 2001
MAMCO, Geneva, 2001
'Drawing Now: Eight Perspectives', Museum of Modern Art, New York, 2002
Albright Knox Gallery, Buffalo, New York, 2003
'Days Like These: The Tate Triennial of Contemporary British Art', Tate Britain, London, 2003
8th International Istanbul Biennial, Istanbul, 2003
'Living Inside the Grid', New Museum of Contemporary Art, New York, 2003
Whitechapel Art Gallery, London, 2004

Select publications
DOLEY, published by Paul Noble, 1995
Cream, Phaidon, London, 1998
Introduction to Nobson Newtown, Salon Verlag, Cologne, 1998
Nobson Central, Verlag der Buchhandlung Walther König, Cologne, 2000

JOÃO PENALVA
b. 1949, Lisbon (Portugal); lives in London (UK) and Berlin (Germany)

Select exhibitions
Centro Cultural de Belém, Lisbon, 1999
Camden Arts Centre, London, 2000
Portuguese Pavilion, Venice Biennale, Venice, 2001
Rooseum Center for Contemporary Art, Malmö, 2002
Sydney Biennial, Sydney, 2002
'Tech/No/Zone', Museum of Contemporary Art, Taipei, Taiwan, 2002
'Process – Landscape', KIASMA, Museum of Contemporary Art, Helsinki, 2003
'The Labyrinthine Effect', Australian Centre for Contemporary Art, Melbourne, 2003
Berlin Biennale 2, 2004

Select publications
Iwona Blazwick et al., *João Penalva*, Centro Cultural de Belém, Lisbon, 1999
João Penalva, *336 PEK*, Frac Languedoc-Roussillon, Montpellier; Camden Arts Centre, London, 2000
Silvia Eiblmyer, *Character and Player*, Galerie im Taxispalais, Innsbruck; Triton Verlag, Vienna, 2000
Guy Brett et al., *João Penalva*, Electa, Milan, 2001
Pedro Lapa, *R.*, Venice Biennale, Instituto de Arte Contemporânea/Ministry of Culture of Portugal, Lisbon, 2001

KATHY PRENDERGAST
b. 1958, Dublin (Ireland); lives in London (UK)

Select exhibitions
Camden Arts Centre, London, 1991
'Inheritance and Transformation', Irish Museum of Modern Art, Dublin, 1991
Royal Festival Hall, London, 1994
Venice Biennale, Venice, 1995
'City Drawings', Art Now Project Room, Tate Gallery, London, 1997
'The End and the Beginning', Irish Museum of Modern Art, Dublin, 1999–2000
'Terra Incognita: Contemporary Artist's Maps and Other Visual Organizing Systems', Sydney Biennial, Sydney, 2002
'The Paradise', Douglas Hyde Gallery, Dublin, 2002–3

Select publications
Kathy Prendergast, Douglas Hyde Gallery, Dublin, 1990
Range, Camden Arts Centre, 1991
Shane Cullen/Kathy Prendergast, Venice Biennale, Venice, 1995
Art Now, Tate Gallery, London, 1997
The End and the Beginning, Irish Museum of Modern Art, Dublin, 1999

JEROEN DE RIJKE/WILLEM DE ROOIJ
Jeroen de Rijke: b. 1970, Brouwershaven (Netherlands); lives in Amsterdam (Netherlands)
Willem de Rooij: b. 1969, Beverwijk (Netherlands); lives in Amsterdam (Netherlands)

Select exhibitions
'Forever and Ever', Galerie Daniel Buchholz, Cologne, 1999
'Anti Memory', Museum of Art, Yokohama, 2000
'Squatters', Fundação de Serralves, Oporto, 2001
'Tre Filmer/Three Films', Museet for Samtidskunst, Oslo, 2001
'Centre of Attraction: 8th Baltic Triennial of International Art', Contemporary Art Centre, Vilnius, 2002
'Tableaux Vivants: Lebende Bilder und Attitüden in Fotografie, Film und Video', Kunsthalle Wien, Vienna, 2002
Villa Arson, Nice, 2002
Kunsthalle Zürich, Zurich, 2003
'Nation', Frankfurter Kunstverein, Frankfurt, 2003
The Douglas Hyde Gallery, Dublin, 2003
'The Point of Departure', Galerie Daniel Buchholz, Cologne, 2003

Select publications
Jeroen de Rijke/Willem de Rooij: After the Hunt, Frankfurter Kunstverein, Frankfurt; Museum Abteiberg, Mönchengladbach; Lukas & Sternberg, New York, 2000
De Rijke/De Rooij: Director's Cut, Museet for Samtidskunst, Oslo, 2001

Eva Meyer-Hermann (ed.), *Jeroen de Rijke & Willem de Rooij: Spaces and Films 1998–2002*, Van Abbemuseum, Eindhoven, 2003

ANRI SALA
b. 1974, Tirana (Albania); lives in Paris (France)

Select exhibitions

'Anri Sala', Stichting De Appel, Amsterdam, 2000
'Manifesta 3', Ljubljana, 2000
'Nocturnes', MAMCO, Geneva, 2000
'Voilà: le monde dans la tête', Musée d'Art Moderne de la Ville de Paris, Paris, 2000
'It Has Been Raining Here', Galerie Chantal Crousel, Paris, 2001
Venice Biennale, Venice, 2001
'Jean-Luc Moulène and Anri Sala', São Paulo Biennial, São Paulo, 2002
Kunsthalle Wien, Vienna, 2003
'Moulène-Sala', Musée des Beaux-Arts, Nantes, France, 2003
Venice Biennale, Venice, 2003
ARC-Musée d'Art Moderne de la Ville de Paris, Paris, 2004
Art Institute of Chicago, Chicago, 2004

Select publications

Edi Muka, *Anri Sala*, Manifesta 3, Ljubljana, 2000
Anri Sala, Stichting De Appel, Amsterdam, 2001
Moulene/Sala, São Paulo Biennial, São Paulo, 2002
Gerald Matt, Hans Ulrich Obrist and Edi Muka, *Anri Sala*, Kunsthalle Wien, Vienna, 2003

YVAN SALOMONE
b. 1957, Saint-Malô (France); lives in Saint-Malô

Select exhibitions

'Dehors, La Criée', Halle d'Art Contemporain, Rennes, 1992
'Off Her Course', Witte de With Center for Contemporary Art, Rotterdam, 1994
'Watt', Witte de With Center for Contemporary Art, Rotterdam, 1994
'Copie' (with Gilles Mahé), Espace Croisé, Lilles, 1996
'I see the sea and the sea sees me', MAMCO, Geneva, 2000
'De Artaud…à Twombly, un choix', Cabinet d'Art Graphique, Centre Georges Pompidou, Paris, 2001
'REPLAY', MAMCO, Geneva, 2002
'Répétitions', Centre d'Art 'Le Spot 1 & 2', Le Havre, 2003

Select publications

Rennes 120, Galerie Joseph Dutertre, Rennes, 1994

Bruxelles 284, Galerie Albert Baronian, Brussels, 1996
Maquis, Le Plateau, Paris, 2002
Répétitions, 'Le Spot 1 & 2', Le Havre, 2003

BOJAN SARCEVIC
b. 1974, Belgrade (Serbia); lives in Berlin (Germany)

Select exhibitions

Manifesta 2, Luxembourg, 1998
Gesellschaft für Aktuelle Kunst, Bremen, 2000
'Ars 01', KIASMA, Museum of Contemporary Art, Helsinki, 2001
Galerie Gebauer, Berlin, 2001
Stedelijk Museum, Amsterdam, 2001
'My head is on fire but my heart is full of love', Charlottenborg, Copenhagen, 2002
'Spirit of Versatility and Inclusiveness', BQ, Cologne, 2002
'Clandestines', Venice Biennale, Venice, 2003
'Déplacements', Musée d'Art Moderne de la Ville de Paris, Paris, 2003
'Verticality Downwards', Kunstverein München, Munich, 2003

Select publications

Worker's Favourite Outfit Worn While S/he Worked, Gesellschaft für Aktuelle Kunst, Bremen, 2000
Spirit of Versatility and Inclusiveness, BQ, Cologne, 2002
La quête du sens se joue entre la verticalité humaine et l'horizon où se perd le chemin, Centre d'Art Contemporain, Brétigny-sur-Orge, 2003

GREGOR SCHNEIDER
b. 1969, Rheydt (Germany); lives in Mönchengladbach-Rheydt (Germany)

Select exhibitions

'16.9.1993', Konrad Fischer Galerie, Düsseldorf, 1993
'Performing Buildings', Tate Gallery, London, 1998
'Totes Haus ur 85–98', Musée d'Art Moderne de la Ville de Paris, Paris, 1998
'Apocalypse', Royal Academy of Arts, London, 2000
'Totes Haus ur', German Pavilion, Venice Biennale, Venice, 2001
'Gregor Schneider', Hamburger Kunsthalle, Hamburg, 2003
'Gregor Schneider', Museum of Contemporary Art, Los Angeles, 2003

Select publications

Raimund Stecker and Ingrid Bacher, *Gregor Schneider 1985–1992*, Impulse Galerie Löhrl, Mönchengladbach, 1992

Julian Heynen, *Gregor Schneider Kunsthalle Bern*, Kunsthalle Bern, Berne, 1996
Udo Kittelmann (ed.), *Gregor Schneider, Totes Haus ur. La Biennale di Venezia 2001*, Hatje Cantz, Ostfildern, 2001
Amine Haase, *Hannelore Reuen–Gregor Schneider*, Hamburger Kunsthalle, Hamburg, 2003

ALLAN SEKULA
b. 1951, Erie, Pennsylvania (USA); lives in Los Angeles (USA)

Select exhibitions

'Dear Bill Gates', Museum Boijmans Van Beuningen, Rotterdam, 2000
'Contemporary Moments', MACBA, Barcelona, 2001
'Open City: Street Photographs Since 1950', Museum of Modern Art, Oxford, 2001
'Titanic's Wake', Galerie Michel Rein, Paris; Centro Cultural de Belém, Lisbon, 2001
'Fish Story', Documenta 11, Kassel, 2002
'The Politics of Place', BildMuseet, Umeå University, Umeå, 2002
'Trade: Waren, Wege und Werte im Welthandel heute', Nederlands Foto Instituut, Rotterdam, 2002
'Performance Under Working Conditions', Generali Foundation, Vienna, 2003

Select publications

Allan Sekula, *Photography against the Grain: Essays and Photo Works 1973–1983*, Press of the Nova Scotia College of Art and Design, Halifax, 1984
Fish Story, Witte de With Center for Contemporary Art, Rotterdam; Richter Verlag, Düsseldorf, 1995
Allan Sekula: Dead Letter Office, Nederlands Foto Instituut, Rotterdam, 1997
Geography Lesson: Canadian Notes, Vancouver Art Gallery, Vancouver; MIT Press, Cambridge, Mass., 1997
Dismal Science: Photo Works 1972–1996, University Galleries, Illinois State University, Normal, Illinois, 1999
Allan Sekula, Titanic's Wake, Le Point du Jour, Liège, 2003
Sabine Breitwieser, Benjamin H. D. Buchloch, Dietrich Karner and Allan Sekula, *Allan Sekula, Performance Under Working Conditions*, Generali Foundation, Vienna, 2003

SHIMABUKU
b. 1969, Kobe (Japan); lives in Yokohama (Japan)

Select exhibitions

'Every Day', Sydney Biennial, Sydney, 1998

'Christmas in the Southern Hemisphere', Air de Paris, France, 1999
'Extra et Ordinaire', Printemps de Cahors, Cahors, 1999
'As It Is', Ikon Gallery, Birmingham, 2000
'Facts of Life', Hayward Gallery, London, 2001
'The Octopus Returns', Kobe Art Village Center/Suma Rikyu Park, Kobe, 2001
'Swansea Jack Memorial Dog Swimming Competition', Glynn Vivian Art Gallery, Swansea, 2003
'Utopia Station', Venice Biennale, Venice, 2003
'Watching the River Flow', Shugoarts, Tokyo, 2003

Select publications
Shimabuku, 'Je voyage avec une sirène de 165 mètres de long', *BLOC NOTES*, no. 17, Autumn 1999
Pascal Beausse, 'Shimabuku', *Flash Art*, no. 208 October 1999
Duncan McLaren, 'Artists on the Move', *Contemporary*, June–August 2002
Elein Fleiss, 'Trains and Boats and Planes', *Purple*, no. 12, Summer 2002

ROSS SINCLAIR
b. 1966, Glasgow (UK); lives in Glasgow

Select exhibitions
'Fortress Real Life', South London Gallery, London, 2001
'Selected Real Life', Badischer Kunstverein, Karlsruhe, 2001–2
Galleria Raffaella Cortese, Milan, 2002
Galerie Yvon Lambert, Paris, 2002
'No one ever dies there, no one has a head', Hartware Medien Kunstverein, Dortmund, 2002
The Agency, London, 2002
'Northern Grammar', Sølvberget – Stavanger Kulturhus, Stavanger, 2003
'Sanctuary', GOMA, Glasgow, 2003
'On Stage', Kunstverein Hannover, Hanover; Villa Merkel, Esslingen, 2003

Select publications
Ross Sinclair: Real Life, Centre for Contemporary Art, Tramway, Pier Arts Centre, Glasgow, 1997
Real Life and How to Live It, Fruitmarket Gallery, Edinburgh, 2000
Northern Grammar, Sølvberget – Stavanger Kulturhus, Stavanger, 2003
On Stage, Kunstverein Hannover, Hanover; Villa Merkel, Esslingen, 2003
If North was South and East was West, Badischer Kunstverein, Karlsruhe, 2004

SIMON STARLING
b. 1967, Epsom (UK); lives in Berlin (Germany)

Select exhibitions
Camden Arts Centre, London, 2000
'CMYK/RGB', Frac Languedoc-Roussillon, Montpellier, 2001
'Inverted Retrograde Theme', Secession, Vienna, 2001
'Djungel', Dundee Contemporary Arts, Dundee, 2002
'Kakteenhaus', Portikus, Frankfurt, 2002
'GNS (Global Navigation System)', Palais de Tokyo, Paris, 2003
'Moving Pictures', Guggenheim, Bilbao, 2003
'The Moderns', Castello di Rivoli, Turin, 2003
'Zenomap', Venice Biennale, Venice, 2003

Select publications
Simon Starling, Camden Arts Centre, London, 2000
CMYK/RGB, Frac Languedoc-Roussillon, Montpellier, 2001
Inverted Retrograde Theme, Secession, Vienna, 2001
Djungel, Dundee Contemporary Arts, Dundee, 2002
Kakteenhaus, Portikus, Frankfurt, 2002

THOMAS STRUTH
b. 1954, Geldern (Germany); lives in Düsseldorf (Germany)

Select exhibitions
'Strangers and Friends', Art Gallery of Ontario, Toronto, 1995
'Invisible Light', Museum of Modern Art, Oxford, 1997
'Portraits', Sprengel Museum, Hanover, 1997
'Thomas Struth STILL', Centre National de la Photographie, Paris; Gallery Shimada, Tokyo; Stedelijk Museum, Amsterdam, 1999
'Thomas Struth: My Portrait', National Museum of Modern Art, Tokyo; National Museum of Art, Kyoto, 2000–1
'Open City: Aspects of Street Photography 1950–2000', Museum of Modern Art, Oxford, 2001
'Passenger: The Viewer as Participant', Astrup Fearnley Museet for Moderne Kunst, Oslo, 2002
'Thomas Struth', Dallas Museum of Art, Dallas; Museum of Contemporary Art, Los Angeles; Metropolitan Museum, New York; Museum of Contemporary Art, Chicago, 2002–3
'Cruel and Tender: The Real in the Twentieth-Century Photograph', Tate Modern, London; Museum Ludwig, Cologne, 2003
'Family Ties', Peabody Essex Museum, Salem, Mass., 2003

Select publications
Thomas Struth, *Unbewusste Orte/Unconscious Places*, Kunsthalle Bern, Berne, 1987

Thomas Struth, *Museum Photographs*, Schirmer/Mosel, Munich, 1993
Thomas Struth, *Strangers and Friends*, Institute of Contemporary Art, Boston, Mass.; Institute of Contemporary Art, London; AGO, Toronto, 1994
Thomas Struth: Still, Carré d'Art, Nîmes; Stedelijk Museum, Amsterdam; Centre National de la Photographie, Paris, 1998
Thomas Struth, *My Portrait*, National Museum of Modern Art, Tokyo; National Museum of Modern Art, Kyoto, 2000
Dieter Schwarz, *Thomas Struth: Dandelion Room*, Distributed Art Publishers Inc., New York in association with Schirmer/Mosel, Munich, 2001
Thomas Struth 1977–2002, Dallas Museum of Art, Dallas; Yale University Press, New Haven and London, 2002

RIRKRIT TIRAVANIJA
b. 1961, Buenos Aires (Argentina); lives in Berlin (Germany)

Select exhibitions
Kunsthalle Basel, Basel, 1995
'Thinking Print', Museum of Modern Art, New York, 1996
'Cities on the Move', Louisiana Museum of Modern Art, Humlebæk; CAPC Bordeaux; Secession, Vienna, 1997–98
'Untitled, 1998 (das soziale kapital)', migros museum – Museum für Gegenwartskunst, Zurich, 1998
'd'APERTutto', Venice Biennale, Venice, 1999
'LKW, Lebenskunstwerke, Kunst in der Stadt 4', Kunsthaus Bregenz, Bregenz, 2000
'Demo Station', Portikus, Frankfurt, 2001
'no fire no ashes', neugerriemschneider, Berlin, 2001
'No Ghost Just a Shell', Kunsthalle Zürich, Zurich, 2002
Secession, Vienna, 2002
'In the future everything will be chrome' (with Nick Relph and Oliver Payne), Gavin Brown Enterprise (Modern), New York, 2003
'Utopia Station', Venice Biennale, Venice, 2003

Select publications
Alexander von Melo et al., *Parkett*, no. 44, 1995
Das soziale Kapital, migros museum – Museum für Gegenwartskunst, Zurich, 1998
Rirkrit Tiravanija: Demo Station, Portikus, Frankfurt, 2001
Rirkrit Tiravanija, Secession, Vienna; Verlag der Buchhandlung Walther König, Cologne, 2002

METTE TRONVOLL
b. 1965, Trondheim (Norway); lives in Berlin (Germany)

Select exhibitions

'Manifesta 1', Rotterdam, 1996
Galerie Max Hetzler, Berlin, 2000
Staatliche Kunsthalle Baden-Baden, Baden-Baden, 2000
'Ars 01', KIASMA, Museum of Contemporary Art, Helsinki, 2001
Galleri K, Oslo, 2001
Museet for Samtidskunst, Oslo, 2001
'Gegenüber', Landesgalerie am Oberösterreichischen Landesmuseum, Salzburg and Linz, 2002
SK Stiftung Kultur, Cologne, 2002
'Spread in Prato', Dryphoto Arte Contemporanea, Prato, 2002
'Beyond Paradise', Fine Art Museum, Shanghai, 2003
'Happiness', Mori Art Museum, Tokyo, 2003

Select publications

Ida Kierulf, 'Mette Tronvoll', European Photography, no. 69, vol. 22, Summer 2001
Timo Valjakka, 'Mette Tronvoll', ARS 01: Unfolding Perspectives, KIASMA, Museum of Contemporary Art, Helsinki, 2001
Pier Luigi Tazzi, Spread in Prato, Dryphoto Arte Contemporanea, Prato, 2002

LUC TUYMANS
b. 1958, Mortsel (Belgium); lives in Antwerp (Belgium)

Select exhibitions

'Superstition', Institute of Contemporary Art, London, 1995
'Premonition: Works on Paper', Kunsthalle Bern, Berne, 1997
'Examining Pictures', Museum of Contemporary Art, Chicago, 1999
'The Carnegie International', Carnegie Museum of Art, Pittsburgh, 1999
'The Purge; Paintings 1991–1998', Bonnefantenmuseum, Maastricht, 1999
'Open Ends', Museum of Modern Art, New York, 2000
Sydney Biennial, Sydney, 2000
Belgian Pavilion, Venice Biennale, Venice, 2001
SMAK, Stedelijk Museum voor Actuele Kunst, Ghent, 2001
'Dear Painter, Paint Me', Centre Georges Pompidou, Paris, 2002
Documenta 11, Kassel, 2002
'The Arena', Kunstverein Hannover, Hanover; Pinakothek der Moderne, Munich; Kunstmuseum, St Gallen, 2003

Select publications

Nancy Spector et al., Luc Tuymans, Phaidon, London, 1996

Premonition. Zeichnungen, Drawings, Kunsthalle Bern, Berne, 1997
Robert Storr, Jan Hoet and Philippe Pirotte, Luc Tuymans: Mwana Kitoko (Beautiful White Man), Belgian Pavilion, Venice Biennale, Venice, 2001
Alison M. Gingeras et al., Dear Painter, Paint Me, Centre Georges Pompidou, Paris, 2002
Mika Hannula, Enrique Juncosa, Gerrit Vermeiren, Luc Tuymans: Display, Centro de Arte de Salamanca, Salamanca, 2003
The Arena, Kunstverein Hannover, Hanover, 2003

DAVID VAUGHAN
b. 1966, Canterbury (UK); lives in Prague (Czech Republic)

David Vaughan has been Editor-in-Chief of Radio Prague, the international service of Czech Radio, for the last five years. Prior to that he was a correspondent for the BBC World Service. He has often written for the Czech and British press, and also produced the documentary film The Second Life of Lidice, made for Czech Television on the 60th anniversary of the Lidice massacre. In 2001 he received the Prix Bohemia, the Czech Republic's main annual radio award, for his radio documentary A Tale of Two Villages.

JANE AND LOUISE WILSON
b. 1967, Newcastle (UK); live in London (UK)

Select exhibitions

'The Carnegie International', Carnegie Museum of Art, Pittsburgh, 1999
'Jane and Louise Wilson', Serpentine Gallery, London, 1999
'Stasi City', Hamburger Kunsthalle, Hamburg, 1999
'Turner Prize Exhibition', Tate Gallery, London, 1999
'Public Offerings', Museum of Contemporary Art, Los Angeles, 2001
Kunst-Werke, Berlin, 2002
'A Free and Anonymous Monument', BALTIC, Gateshead, 2003
'Moving Pictures', Guggenheim Museum, Bilbao, 2003
'New Acquisitions', Museum of Modern Art, New York, 2003

Select publications

Normapaths, Chisenhale Gallery, London, 1995
Stasi City, Kunstverein Hannover, Hanover, 1997
Peter Schjeldahl et al., Jane and Louise Wilson, Serpentine Gallery, London, 1999
Jeremy Millar and Claire Doherty, Jane and Louise Wilson, Ellipsis, London, 2001
A Free and Anonymous Monument, BALTIC, Gateshead, 2003

CERITH WYN EVANS
b. 1958, Llanelli (UK); lives in London (UK)

Select exhibitions

'Inverse Reverse Perverse', White Cube/Jay Jopling, London, 1996
'Cerith Wyn Evans', Deitch Projects, New York, 1997
'Cerith Wyn Evans', Galerie Daniel Buchholz, Cologne, 2001
'Cerith Wyn Evans', Kunsthaus Glarus, Glarus, 2001
'Cerith Wyn Evans', Galerie Georg Kargl, Vienna, 2001
'La Ville, le Jardin, la Mémoire 1998–2000', French Academy at Rome, Villa Medici, Rome, 2001
'The Greenhouse Effect', Serpentine Gallery (in collaboration with The Natural History Museum), London, 2001
Documenta 11, Kassel, 2002
'Iconoclash: Image Wars in Science, Religion and Art', ZKM, Karlsruhe, 2002
'My head is on fire but my heart is full of love', Charlottenborg, Copenhagen, 2002
'Cardinales', MARCO, Vigo, 2003
'Cerith Wyn Evans', Galerie Neu, Berlin, 2003
'Cerith Wyn Evans', mini MATRIX, Berkeley Art Museum, San Francisco, 2003

Select publications

Material Culture, Hayward Gallery, London, 1997
Sensation, Royal Academy of Arts, London, 1997
Cerith Wyn Evans, CCA, Kitakyushu, 1998
Francesco Bonami and Hans Ulrich Obrist, Dreams, Fondazione Sandretto Re Rebaudengo Per L'Arte, Turin, 1999
Simon Morley, The Greenhouse Effect, Serpentine Gallery, London (in collaboration with the Natural History Museum), 2000
Alex Farquharson, Wales: Unauthorized Versions, part of 'Welsh Days Festival' organized by the British Council, Croatian Association of Artists, Zagreb, 2001
Documenta 11_ Platform 5: Exhibition, Hatje Cantz, Ostfildern, 2002

FURTHER READING

Yves Abrioux, *Ian Hamilton Finlay: A Visual Primer* (London: Reaktion Books, 1992)

Malcolm Andrews, *Landscape and Western Art* (Oxford: Oxford University Press, 1999)

Malcolm Andrews, *The Search for the Picturesque* (Stanford: Stanford University Press, 1989)

Arjun Appadurai, *Modernity at Large: Cultural Dimensions of Globalization* (Minneapolis: University of Minnesota Press, 1996)

Marc Augé, *Non-Places: Introduction to an Anthropology of Supermodernity*, trans. John Howe (London: Verso, 1995)

Gaston Bachelard, *The Poetics of Space* (Boston: Beacon Press, 1994)

Jonathan Bate, *The Song of the Earth* (London: Picador, 2000)

Victor Burgin, *In/Different Spaces: Places and Memory in Visual Culture* (Berkeley, Los Angeles and London: University of California Press, 1996)

Edward S. Casey, *Remembering: A Phenomenological Study* (Bloomington and Indianapolis: Indiana University Press, 2000)

Edward S. Casey, *Getting Back into Place: Towards a Renewed Understanding of the Place-World* (Bloomington and Indianapolis: Indiana University Press, 1993)

Edward S. Casey, *The Fate of Place: A Philosophical History* (Berkeley, Los Angeles and London: University of California Press, 1998)

Edward S. Casey, *Representing Place: Landscape Painting and Maps* (Minneapolis and London: University of Minnesota Press, 2002)

Iain Chambers, *Migrancy, Culture, Identity* (London and New York: Routledge, 1994)

Leo Charney, *Empty Moments: Cinema, Modernity and Drift* (Durham, N.C. and London: Duke University Press, 1998)

David B. Clarke (ed.), *The Cinematic City* (London and New York: Routledge, 1997)

James Clifford, *Routes: Travel and Translation in the Late Twentieth Century* (Cambridge, Mass. and London: Harvard University Press, 1997)

Mike Crang and Nigel Thrift (eds.), *Thinking Space* (London: Routledge, 2000)

Gilles Deleuze, *Desert Islands and Other Texts 1953–1974* (Los Angeles and New York: Semiotext(e), 2004)

Gilles Deleuze and Félix Guattari, *A Thousand Plateaus*, trans. Brian Massumi (London: Athlone Press, 1988)

J. Nicholas Entrikin, *The Betweenness of Place: Towards a Geography of Modernity* (Basingstoke and London: Macmillan, 1991)

Alec Finlay (ed.), *Wood Notes Wild: Essays on the Poetry and Art of Ian Hamilton Finlay* (Edinburgh: Polygon, 1995)

Dolores Hayden, *The Power of Place: Urban Landscapes and Public History* (Cambridge, Mass. and London: MIT Press, 1997)

John Brinckerhoff Jackson, *Discovering the Vernacular Landscape* (New Haven and London: Yale University Press, 1984)

Caren Kaplan, *Questions of Travel: Postmodern Discourses of Displacement* (Durham, N.C. and London: Duke University Press, 1996)

Stephen Kern, *The Culture of Time and Space 1880–1918* (Cambridge, Mass.: Harvard University Press, 1983)

Robert Pogue Harrison, *Forests: The Shadow of Civilization* (Chicago and London: University of Chicago Press, 1992)

Martin Heidegger, *Basic Writings*, ed. David Farrell Krell (London: Routledge, 1993)

Nick Huggett (ed.), *Space from Zeno to Einstein: Classic Readings with a Contemporary Commentary* (Cambridge, Mass. and London: MIT Press, 1999)

Max Jammer, *Concepts of Space: The History of Theories of Space in Physics* (Cambridge, Mass.: Harvard University Press, 1970)

François Jullien, *The Propensity of Things: Towards a History of Efficacy in China*, trans. Janet Lloyd (New York: Zone Books, 1999)

Joseph Leo Koerner, *Caspar David Friedrich and the Subject of Landscape* (London: Reaktion Books, 1990)

Henri Lefebvre, *The Production of Space*, trans. Donald Nicholson-Smith (Oxford and Cambridge, Mass.: Blackwell, 1991)

Scott MacDonald, *The Garden in the Machine: A Field Guide to Independent Films about Place* (Berkeley, Los Angeles and London: University of California Press, 2001)

Alberto Manguel and Gianni Guadalupi, *The Dictionary of Imaginary Places* (London: Bloomsbury, 1999)

Doreen Massey, *Space, Place and Gender* (Cambridge: Polity Press, 1994)

D. W. Meinig (ed.), *The Interpretation of Ordinary Landscapes* (Oxford: Oxford University Press, 1979)

Edwin T. Morris, *The Gardens of China: History, Art and Meaning* (New York: Scribner's, 1983)

Max Oeschlaeger, *The Idea of Wilderness: From Prehistory to the Age of Ecology* (New Haven and London: Yale University Press, 1991)

Georges Perec, *Species of Spaces and Other Pieces*, trans. John Sturrock, Harmondsworth: Penguin, 1997)

Simon Pugh, *Garden – Nature – Language* (Manchester: Manchester University Press, 1988)

Hans Reichenbach, *The Philosophy of Time and Space* (New York: Dover, 1958)

Simon Schama, *Landscape and Memory* (London: Harper Collins, 1995)

John Rennie Short, *Global Dimensions: Space, Place and the Contemporary World* (London: Reaktion Books, 2001)

Edward W. Soja, *Thirdspace: Journeys to Los Angeles and Other Real-and-Imagined Places* (Oxford and Cambridge, Mass.: Blackwell, 1996)

Andrei Tarkovsky, *Collected Screenplays*, trans. William Powell and Natasha Synessios (London: Faber and Faber, 1999)

Anthony Vidler, *The Architectural Uncanny: Essays in the Modern Unhomely* (Cambridge, Mass. and London: MIT Press, 1996)

Paul Virilio, *Speed and Politics*, trans. Mark Polizzotti (New York: Semiotext(e), 1986)

Margaret Wertheim, *The Pearly Gates of Cyberspace: A History of Space from Dante to the Internet* (London: Virago, 1999)

ILLUSTRATION LIST

Measurements are given in centimetres, followed by inches, height before width before depth.

1 Mette Tronvoll, *Ger 002*, 2003 (detail). C-print. Courtesy the artist and Galerie Max Hetzler. Copyright Mette Tronvoll.

2–3 Peter Fischli and David Weiss, *Untitled*, 1997/2000 (detail). Courtesy the artists/Galerie Eva Presenhuber, Zurich

4–5 Stephen Hughes, *Oviedo, Spain*, 2000 (detail). C-print, 102 x 126 (40 ^{1}/$_8$ x 49 ^{5}/$_8$). Courtesy Galerie Thomas Zander, Cologne

6 Shimabuku, *Seafaring Japan*, 2001. Yokohama 2001. Courtesy the artist

10 Andrei Tarkovsky, *Stalker*, 1979. Film still. Courtesy British Film Institute.

12 (left) Vitaly Komar and Alex Melamid, *The People's Choice: Kenya's Most Wanted*, 1996. Oil on canvas, 66 x 96.5 (26 x 38). Courtesy Ronald Feldman Fine Arts, New York

12 (right) Vitaly Komar and Alex Melamid, *The People's Choice: Iceland's Most Wanted*, 1995. Oil on canvas, 40.6 x 66 (16 x 26). Courtesy Ronald Feldman Fine Arts, New York

17 Caspar David Friedrich, *Chasseur in the Forest*, 1813–14. Oil on canvas, 65.7 x 46.7 (25 ^{7}/$_8$ x 18 ^{3}/$_8$). Private collection

19 Ian Hamilton Finlay with Nicholas Sloan, (above left and below right) *Little Sparta: 'The Present Order'*, 1983; (above right) *Little Sparta: 'A Cottage, a Field, a Plough'*. Photographs by Robin Gillanders. Courtesy the artist.

22 Douglas Huebler, *Location Piece #2*. Photowork, 1969. Copyright Douglas Huebler Estate & Multiples Inc, New York

24 Marine Hugonnier, *Ariana*, 2002. Super 16 mm film. 18 min. 36 sec.

26 Guy Moreton, *Wittgenstein's Cottage*, 2002–4. C-print, 40 x 50 (15 ^{3}/$_4$ x 19 ^{5}/$_8$)

29 Doug Aitken, *Electric Earth*, 1999 (production still). Courtesy Victoria Miro Gallery, London; 303 Gallery, New York; Galerie Eva Presenhuber, Zurich

31 Dominique Gonzalez-Foerster, *Plages*, 2001. 35 mm film. 15 min. Original language: Portuguese. Shot in Rio de Janeiro in December 2000. Anna Sanders Films/Le Fresnoy. Copyright the artist

32–33 Jane and Louise Wilson, *A Free and Anonymous Monument*, 2003. A BALTIC/Film and Video Umbrella co-commission. Supported by the National Touring Programme of Arts Council England, Film London and The Henry Moore Foundation. Photos Jerry Hardman-Jones. Courtesy the artists and Lisson Gallery

34–35 Liam Gillick, *Pain in a Building*, 1999 (detail). Courtesy the artist and Corvi-Mora, London

37 Dan Graham, *Homes for America*, 1966. Photo offset reproduction of layout for magazine article, 60.3 x 49.5 (23 ^{3}/$_4$ x 19 ^{1}/$_2$). Courtesy the artist and Marian Goodman Gallery, New York

39 Bojan Sarcevic, *Untitled (Bangkok)*, 2002. 7 min. video, colour & sound. Courtesy BQ, Cologne

41 Stan Douglas, *Le Détroit*, 1999–2000. 35 mm film installation for two 35-mm film projectors, looping device, anamorphic lens, one screen. Dimensions vary with installation. Courtesy of David Zwirner, New York

42–43 Jeroen de Rijke and Willem de Rooij, *Bantar Gebang, Bekasi, West Java, May 2000*. Courtesy of Galerie Daniel Buchholz, Cologne

45 Thomas Struth, *Jiangxi Zhong Lu, Shanghai*, 1996. C-print, edition of 10, 89 x 112 (35 x 44⅛). Courtesy of the artist and Marian Goodman, New York

48 Thomas Struth, *Huang Shan, Huang Shan*, 2002. C-print. Courtesy of the artist and Marian Goodman, New York

50–51 A. K. Dolven, *looking back*, 2000. 3 high-speed, 300 fps 16-mm films on DVD. Camera: Vegar Moen. Courtesy carlier | gebauer, Berlin and Wilkinson Gallery, London. Copyright the artist

53 Simon Starling, *Island for Weeds (Prototype)*, 2003. 'Zenomap', 50th International Exhibition of Art, Venice Biennale, Venice, Italy, 2003. Courtesy The Modern Institute, Glasgow. Photo Jerry Hardman-Jones. Copyright Simon Starling

54–55 Olafur Eliasson, *Moss valley series*, 2002 (detail). 16 C-prints, each 28 x 42 (11 x 16 ^{1}/$_2$). Courtesy neugerriemschneider, Berlin and Tanya Bonakdar Gallery, New York. Copyright the artist

57 Pierre Huyghe, *L'expédition scintillante, Act 1, Untitled (ice boat)*, 2002. Mixed-media installation. Courtesy of the artist and Marian Goodman, New York and Paris

59 Roni Horn, *Becoming a Landscape*, 1999–2001 (detail), 20 images: C-printed photographs. 14 sheets: 77.5 x 58.5 (30 ^{1}/$_2$ x 23). 6 sheets: 52 x 52 (20 ^{1}/$_2$ x 20 ^{1}/$_2$). Courtesy the artist and Matthew Marks Gallery, New York

60 Roni Horn, *Her, Her, Her, and Her (2)*, 2002. Black and white photographs printed on paper, coated with light-sensitive emulsion. 64 images, each 30.5 x 30.5 (12 x 12) glued to one piece: 8 x 8 units. Overall dimension: 244 x 244 (96 x 96). Courtesy the artist and Matthew Marks Gallery, New York

62–63 Graham Gussin, *Remote Viewer*, 2002. Courtesy the artist and Lisson Gallery. Commissioned by Film and Video Umbrella. Copyright Graham Gussin.

65 Adam Chodzko, *Better Scenery* (Detail: Arizona Desert, USA; Sainsbury's Car Park, Finchley Road, London), 2001, Mixed media installation. Commissioned by Camden Art Centre, London. Courtesy the artist.

66 Adam Chodzko, *Better Scenery* (Detail: Grizedale Forest, Cumbria, UK; Italdesign factory, Torino, Italy), 2001. Mixed media installation. Courtesy the artist.

67 Adam Chodzko, *Better Scenery* (Detail: Angel Mews, Islington, London, UK; Fargo,

North Dakota, USA), 2002. Mixed media installation. Courtesy the artist.

69–70 Gregor Schneider, *Totes Haus ur*, 2001. Courtesy Konrad Fischer Galerie. Copyright Gregor Schneider/VG Bildkunst Bonn

73 (top) Liz Arnold, *Melt*, 2000. Acrylic on canvas, 82 x 173 (32 1/4 x 68 1/8). Courtesy Evelyn G. Arnold. Copyright the Estate of Liz Arnold

73 (bottom) Liz Arnold, *Island*, 1999. Acrylic on canvas. Courtesy Evelyn G. Arnold. Copyright the Estate of Liz Arnold

74 Liz Arnold, *Brunettes*, 2000. Acrylic on canvas, 133 x 153 (52 3/8 x 60 1/4). Courtesy Evelyn G. Arnold. Copyright the Estate of Liz Arnold

75 Liz Arnold, *Long Distance*, 2000. Acrylic on canvas, 82 x 127 (32 1/4 x 50). Courtesy Evelyn G. Arnold. Copyright the Estate of Liz Arnold

76–77 Bodys Isek Kingelez, *New Manhattan City 3021*, 2001–2002. Plywood, paper, cardboard, plastic, ink and various materials, 205 x 300 x 280 (80 3/4 x 118 1/8 x 110 1/4). Photo Patrick Gries Copyright C.A.A.C. The Pigozzi Collection, Geneva

78–79 Paul Noble, *Unified Nobson*, 2001. DVD for projection. 3 min. loop. Courtesy Maureen Paley Interim Art, London

80 Rod Dickinson, diagrams and cuttings taken from crop circle researchers and enthusiasts' pamphlets, 1997

81 Rod Dickinson, *Crop Formation, Silbury Hill, Wiltshire*, 1997. Photo Steve Alexander

82 Rod Dickinson, *Crop Formation, Woodborough Hill, Wiltshire*, 2000

84 Dorothy Cross, (top) *Handball Alleys, St Enda's College, Galway, Ireland*, 1999; (bottom) *Poll na bPéist (The Worm's Hole), Inismór, Aran Islands, Co. Galway, Ireland*, 1999. Photos Dorothy Cross

85 Dorothy Cross, *Chiasm*, 1999. Film still. Tenor: Eugene Ginty. Soprano: Carol Smith. Commissioned by the Project Art Centre, Dublin

87 Juan Cruz, *Application for Planning Permit: Proposal to Build a Metaphor*, 2001. Sandridge Railway Bridge, Southbank. Courtesy the artist and Matt's Gallery, London

89 João Penalva, *336 PEK (336 Rivers)*, 1998. Video, 60 min. 52 sec., colour, sound. Courtesy of the artist and Galerie Volker Diehl, Berlin. Copyright João Penalva.

91–93 Joachim Koester, *Bialowieza Forest*, 2001. C-prints, 101 x 126 (39 3/4 x 49 5/8). Courtesy Galleri Nicolai Wallner, Copenhagen

95 Maurizio Cattelan, *Hollywood*, 2001. Colour print, plexiglas, wooden frame, 180 x 400.1 x 14.9 (70 7/8 x 157 1/2 x 5 7/8). Courtesy the artist and Marian Goodman Gallery, New York

97 Cerith Wyn Evans, *Firework Text (Pasolini)*, 1998. Super 16mm film. Duration: 15 minutes. Copyright the artist. Courtesy Jay Jopling/White Cube, London

98–99 Rodney Graham, *Aberdeen*, 2000 (details). Multimedia installation, including slide projection and sound. 20 minutes. Edition of three and one Artist's Proof. Courtesy Donald Young Gallery, Chicago

100 Alexander and Susan Maris, *therapeuticum*, 2002–20 (detail). Courtesy of the artists.

101 Alexander and Susan Maris, *N-56·38·26*, 2002–20. Courtesy of the artists.

103 Luc Tuymans, *The Mission*, 2000. Oil on canvas. 84 x 130 (33 x 51 1/8). From the *Mwana Kitoko* series. Courtesy David Zwirner, New York and Galerie Zeno X, Antwerp

107 Jeremy Deller, *The Battle of Orgreave*, 2001. Commissioned by Artangel. Copyright Jeremy Deller

109 Thomas Demand, *Hof/Yard*, 2002. 35mm film. Courtesy Victoria Miro Gallery, London. Copyright Thomas Demand/VG Bildkunst Bonn

111 Sharon Lockhart, *Teatro Amazonas*, 1999. Film still. Copyright Sharon Lockhart. Courtesy neugerriemschneider, Berlin

113 Anri Sala, *Dammi i colori*, 2003. Colour film with sound – DVD. 15 min. 24 sec. Courtesy Galerie Chantal Crousel, Paris and the artist. Copyright Anri Sala.

115 Katrin von Maltzahn, *Hellersdorf Story*, 1999–2001. Acknowledgments: Tom Nicholson. Copyright Katrin von Maltzahn

116–17 Willie Doherty, *Extracts from a File*, 2000. 5 black-and-white photographs on aluminium. Edition of 6. Courtesy Kerlin Gallery, Dublin

118 Susan Hiller, *Judengasse, Pretzfeld*. From *The J-Street Project*, 2002–3. Copyright the artist

119 Susan Hiller, (top left) *Judengasse, Altenburg*; (top right) *Jüdenstrasse, Weissenfels*; (bottom left) *Judengraben, Kronach*; (bottom right) *Judenhain, Marienburg*. From *The J-Street Project*, 2002–3. Copyright the artist

121 Nathan Coley, *Fourteen Churches of Münster*, 2000. Video still. Commissioned by the Westfälischer Kunstverein, Münster. Copyright the artist

123–25 Jun Nguyen-Hatsushiba, *Memorial Project Nha Trang, Vietnam: Towards the Complex – For the Courageous, the Curious, and the Cowards*, 2001. DVD still, digital video. Courtesy Yokohama Triennale 2001, Mizuma Art Gallery and the artist. Copyright the artist

127 Steve McQueen, *Caribs' Leap/Western Deep*, 2002. *Caribs' Leap*: 14 min., looped, silent. *Western Deep*: 24 min., sound. Courtesy the artist and Marian Goodman Gallery, New York

128–29, 132 Film stills from *The Silent Village*, 1943. Courtesy the British Film Institute

130 *Wynne Horák, Pavla Nešporová and Anna Nešporová by the ruins of the Horák farmhouse*, 2001. Copyright Pavel Štingl

131 *Anna Nešporová, with David Vaughan in her*

house in Lidice, 2001. Copyright Pavel Štingl

135 Ross Sinclair, *Journey to the Edge of the World – The New Republic of St Kilda*, 1999. Courtesy The Agency Contemporary Art, London and Raffaella Cortese, Milan

137 Ross Sinclair, *Real Life and How to Live it, No. 1 – Geography*, 2000. Courtesy The Agency Contemporary Art, London and Raffaella Cortese, Milan

139 Chantal Akerman, *From the Other Side*, 2002. Multi-screen installation. Courtesy the artist and Frith Street Gallery, London

141–43 Kathy Prendergast, *Lost*, 1999. Digital print (ed. 2/25), 85 x 132 (33 $^1/_2$ x 52). Courtesy Kerlin Gallery, Dublin

144 Leif Elggren and Carl Michael von Hausswolff, *The Kingdoms of Elgaland-Vargaland (KREV) physical territory: Svinesund, on the border between Sweden and Norway*, 1999. Copyright the artists

145 Leif Elggren and Carl Michael von Hausswolff, *In conjunction with the 'Utopia Station', a part of the 50th International Art Exhibition of the Biennale di Venezia 2003, we annex and incorporate Utopia within the concept of The Kingdoms of Elgaland-Vargaland (KREV)*. Copyright the artists.

147 Mette Tronvoll, (top left) *Ger 001*, 2003; (top right) *Ger 002*, 2003; (bottom left) *Ger 003*, 2003; (bottom right) *The Purews, Luwsansharaws and Dulamsuren Otschir*, 2003. C-prints. Courtesy the artist and Galerie Max Hetzler. Copyright Mette Tronvoll.

151 Francis Alÿs, *Cuando la fe mueve montañas, Lima, Perú, April 11, 2002 (When Faith Moves Mountains, Lima, Peru, April 11, 2002)*. Still of video installation. Courtesy Galerie Peter Kilchmann, Zurich. Copyright the artist

153 Janet Cardiff, *The Missing Voice (case study b)*, 1999. Audiowalk. Commissioned by Artangel, London.

154–55 Rirkrit Tiravanija, *Untitled (Demonstration No. 3)*, 2001. Installation. Van, diverse utensils, 8 monitors. On the videos there were sequences of the artist's journey. Courtesy neugerriemschneider, Berlin. Copyright the artist

157 Shimabuku, *Cucumber Journey*, 2000. Ikon Gallery, Birmingham. Photos Noguchi Rika. Courtesy the artist & Air de Paris, Paris. Copyright the artist

159–62 All photographs courtesy Hyogo Prefectural Museum of Modern Art, 1995

165 Allan Sekula, *Project for Yokohama*, 2001

167 Yvan Salomone, (top left) *0336. 3. 1099 [blocsusbloc]*, 1999; (centre left) *0392. 5. 0301 [zwangsideen]*; (bottom left) *0357. 4. 0400 [portbaniger]*, 2000; (top right) *0362. 2. 0600 [colimassive]*, 2000; (centre right) *0397. 2. 0501 [stimmestumm]*, 2001; (bottom right) *0375. 1. 1100 [cyndycrawfo]*, 2000. Watercolour, 104 x 145 (41 x 57 $^1/_8$). Copyright Yvan Salomone. Courtesy Galerie Praz-Delavallade, Paris

169 Peter Fischli and David Weiss, (top left) *Untitled*, 1998/2000; (middle left) *Untitled (Berlin Tegel)*, 1991/1992; (bottom left) *Untitled (Tokyo)*, 1990/2003; (top right) *Untitled*, 1988/2000; (middle right) *Untitled (Rio Air France Jumbo)*, 1989/1998; (bottom right) *Untitled (Amsterdam Esso)*, 1998/2000. C-prints. Courtesy the artists/Galerie Eva Presenhuber, Zurich

170 Peter Fischli and David Weiss, (top left) *Untitled (London British Air)*, 1997/2000; (middle left) *Untitled (Frankfurt Condor)*, 1998/2000; (bottom left) *Untitled*, 1997/2000; (top right) *Untitled (London Air Europe)* 1988/2000; (middle right) *Untitled*, 1990/2000; (bottom right), *Untitled*, 1999/2000. C-prints. Courtesy the artists/Galerie Eva Presenhuber, Zurich

173 Stephen Hughes, (top left) *South of Estepona*, 1999; (top right) *Famara, Lanzarote*, 1999; (bottom left) *Malaga 1, Spain*, 1999; (bottom right) *Swanley, England*, 1997. All C-type prints, 126 x 102 (50 x 40). Courtesy Galerie Thomas Zander, Cologne

174–76 Boris Mikhailov, *TV-Mania* series, 1991–2002. Colour photographs, size variable. Courtesy Galerie Barbara Weiss, Berlin. Copyright the artist

INDEX OF ARTISTS

Page numbers in *italics* refer to illustrations